UNDERGROUND

Official Handbook

Bob Bayman

Capital Transport

Preface

The London Underground is one of the world's best known transport systems. It is used extensively by Londoners and all who visit London. The diagrammatic map, the bar and circle symbol and the distinctive trains and stations are uniquely associated with the capital's metropolitan rail system. Even so, many of the Underground's lifelong users have little idea of what goes on to make it work, how its equipment operates or the historical background to the world's first urban railway. This book is a short guide around the system and gives answers to many of the questions often asked about London's Underground.

ISBN 978-1-85414-317-4

Published by Capital Transport Publishing
PO Box 250, Harrow, Middlesex

Printed by CT Printing Ltd

© Capital Transport Publishing 2008

Sixth edition

All photographs are © Capital Transport Publishing
except those supplied by the following:

Ian Bell 47, 58
Bombardier 32, 35, 75
Brian Hardy 8 bottom, 28, 31 top, 33, 34, 37 top, 60, 68
London Transport Museum 7 bottom left, 9 top, 12 top, 13 top
London Underground Ltd 74, 77
Kim Rennie 30, 36, 37 bottom

Contents

# UNDERGROUND Introduction

Below left Piccadilly Circus – once popularly known as 'the Hub of the Empire'. A Bakerloo line train enters the station.

Right The interior of a Circle line train – the closely spaced doorways give this stock excellent ability to carry large numbers of passengers over short distances.

The total length of route served by Underground trains is 410 km (255miles) Of this total, 56% is in the open, 37% in tube tunnel and 7% in cut and cover.

Each day over 3 million journeys are made on the Underground. After a long decline between 1949 and the early 1980s, demand then began to increase sharply (by more than 70 per cent in the following six years). The early 1990s brought a shallow reduction in work-related traffic because of economic recession, but recovery followed and the since the mid-1990s most years have seen existing records broken as the busiest years ever on the Underground. Setbacks following international events, even after terrorist action on the system itself in 2005, were quickly recovered.

Culturally London had changed. Growth in retailing and leisure activity in the 1980s was followed by the rise of London as a global centre of business and tourism, causing much of the increased travel demand at times of the day and week traditionally regarded as 'off-peak'.

Rapid improvements in technology and comfort in homes, road transport and the workplace had also raised customer expectations of the travelling environment. Through the 1990s the Underground made enormous progress in meeting these demands. In the wake of the fire at King's Cross station in 1987, safety had become the subject of systematic management techniques; the focus then turned to issues of quality and efficiency. The result was that during the 1990s, in addition to carrying much increased numbers, the system also reduced accidents of all kinds, substantially increased customer satisfaction and increased its 'operating surplus' from zero to nearly £300 million per year, by the end of the decade this money contributing over 40 per cent of the investment in renewals and improvements.

Reliance on Government funding was, however, a major problem. Cash availability for investment was not only restricted as the rising cost of healthcare and education drained public resources, but was variable at short notice – making it increasingly difficult to plan for major

Greater London is home to over 7 million people of rich cultural diversity, occupying some 618 square miles. As Europe's leading financial services provider, it is a source of wealth to the entire nation, and has itself an economy greater than that of Hong Kong, or Austria, or Greece. London's buoyant economy attracts a vast workforce from within its own boundaries, and from a surprisingly large catchment area extending well over one hundred miles in most directions. Some 10 per cent of London's surface area is given over to highways, compared with about 25 per cent of a typical North American city, making it particularly dependent on railways for moving about.

infrastructure renewal – and tied to each individual fiscal year, leading to waste and a focus on short term work. The combined effect of these circumstances had meant that only in two or three years since the 1950s had enough been spent to adequately replace worn out equipment. It was clear that the improving performance of the system could not be sustained unless this problem was tackled.

To support publicly owned enterprise, an alternative source of funding was developed in the form of the 'Private Finance Initiative', which allowed private sector investment, and which the Underground was quick to exploit. The first scheme was for the supply of a computer service at the Canary Wharf offices, but the next was much more significant, providing a new fleet of trains to the Northern line, which could not be afforded by normal funding. Others to follow were for power supplies, a new communications system and for the extension of the Piccadilly line to the then proposed Terminal 5 at Heathrow Airport.

In 1998 the new Government announced its intention to extend this principle to all the system's assets, by inviting bids for the network's engineering from the private sector, in an initiative known as 'Private-Public Partnership' (PPP). This plan reached fruition in 2003 with the award of three contracts to two private sector consortia, Metronet gaining two (the Subsurface lines; and Bakerloo, Central, Victoria and Waterloo & City lines) and Tube Lines one (Jubilee, Northern and Piccadilly).

The operation of the lines remained in public ownership, but from July 2003 responsibility was transferred from central government to Transport for London, part of the Greater London Authority and accountable to the elected Mayor. Given difficult experiences with the earlier privatisation of British Rail, particular emphasis was placed on maintaining safety through the organisational transition, and enhancing it thereafter. The new arrangements were intended to provide the investment needed to improve the quality of service and capacity to meet the increasing needs of London over the first three decades of the new century, and ensure that this vital support to the region's economy could be sustained.

The new arrangements were controversial, and became the focus of much political wrangling and media attention. Much good did come from privatisation of maintenance and renewals, and gradually standards of service and cleanliness began to improve. However, Metronet in particular came under heavy criticism from all quarters for poor delivery, and in 2007 went into administration under the burden of increasing financial difficulty. In 2008 TfL itself took over the business of Metronet, leaving only the Jubilee, Northern and Piccadilly lines maintained under the original PPP concept.

History

Below Baker Street Hammersmith & City and Circle lines with some of the original 1863 elements restored.

The first underground railway in the world started operating when the Metropolitan Railway opened a line between Bishops Road, Paddington and Farringdon on 10th January 1863. At the Paddington end there was a connection to the Great Western Railway and, during the first few months of operation, the Great Western loaned locomotives and rolling stock to the Metropolitan. After one of the disputes which characterised the relationship between the two companies for many years, the Great Western withdrew its rolling stock and the Metropolitan prevailed upon the Great Northern Railway company to help it out until stock of its own could be built. By July 1864 the Metropolitan had enough of its own stock to operate the service without assistance.

Specially designed steam locomotives were ordered from Beyer Peacock of Manchester, fitted with a system for condensing the exhaust steam to reduce the smoke appearing in the tunnels. The locomotives were of the 4-4-0 tank engine type and they became the standard for both the Metropolitan and District Railways. An example of one of them has survived to be preserved in the London Transport Museum.

After the opening of the initial section in 1863, there were various extensions to the east and the line reached Aldgate in 1876. It was further extended round to a station called Tower of London (on the site of the present Tower Hill) in 1882. A westward projection was started from a junction at Praed Street between the

Left Although the steam locomotives employed by the Metropolitan and Metropolitan District railways were designed to consume their own smoke by diverting it into the engine's water tanks, in practice they needed to be able to expel it as frequently as possible. Therefore ventilation shafts were built from the tunnel roofs to the outside, usually into the squares or gardens above. This ventilation aperture remains at Great Portland Street station.

Below left Steam locomotive No. 55 pulling a train to Hammersmith shortly before being replaced by electric trains in 1905. Engine No. 23 of similar appearance is preserved at the LT Museum.

Below right Map produced by the Metropolitan Railway in 1882 showing the Inner Circle line complete in all but the section between Liverpool Street and Tower Hill. Parliament had to intervene to compel the Met and District railways to complete the link.

stations at Paddington and Edgware Road. This line passed through a new Paddington station built exclusively for the Metropolitan (the present Circle/District line station), proceeded south to High Street Kensington and then curved east to South Kensington, which was reached in 1868.

At this point a second underground railway company entered the story. This was the Metropolitan District Railway, usually referred to as the District. The District built the southern section of the present-day Circle line between South Kensington and Mansion House, opening it in stages between 1868 and 1871. The present Embankment along the north shore of the Thames was built during this period as part of the construction of the District's tunnels between Westminster and Temple.

The final part of the Circle was opened in 1884 when the joint construction by the Metropolitan and District of the link between Mansion House and the Tower was completed.

The project included an extension to Whitechapel and a triangular junction with the present-day Circle line between Liverpool Street, Aldgate East and the Tower.

Both the District and Metropolitan became involved in the construction or operation of extensions radiating from the Circle line. Jointly with the Great Western, the Metropolitan operated a branch to Hammersmith which was opened in 1864. This line, like the first section of the Circle to Farringdon, was constructed to take the Great Western's broad gauge rolling stock. The track was laid as mixed gauge to allow both 4ft 8½in and 7ft 0½in gauge rolling stock to operate. Traces of this can still be seen today in the wide gaps between tracks on the Hammersmith branch and the generous tunnel clearances between Paddington and Farringdon.

The District reached Hammersmith in 1874 and then built a further short extension to a junction with the London & South Western Railway at Studland Road near what is now Ravenscourt Park station. This gave the District access to Richmond to which point it began running trains in 1877.

In 1879 it opened an extension from Turnham Green to Ealing Broadway.

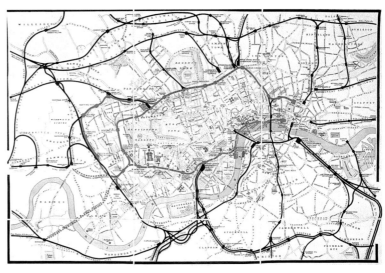

Right The Metropolitan Railway's lines running through north west London, Middlesex, Hertfordshire and Buckinghamshire followed the practice of other main line railways. This called for signalling systems designed to handle freight as well as passenger trains. A few signal boxes still exist, as does this one at Chesham.

Below Kennington was built as one of the City & South London stations, but was greatly expanded when the Charing Cross, Euston & Hampstead Railway was extended to form a junction with the original line in 1926.

In the following year the branch to West Brompton (opened 1869) was extended to Putney Bridge and, following the construction of a bridge across the river to connect with the London & South Western Railway at East Putney, District trains reached Wimbledon in 1889.

During this period the Metropolitan was also expanding. Apart from the line to Hammersmith already mentioned, a branch from Baker Street to Swiss Cottage was opened in 1868. This was extended to Willesden Green in 1879 and to Harrow-on-the-Hill in 1880. Pinner was reached in 1885, Rickmansworth in 1887 and Chesham in 1889.

All the services on the Metropolitan and District Railways were originally steam operated, the District using the same 4-4-0 condensing tank locomotives as the Metropolitan. The District had 4-wheeled wooden carriages, usually formed into 9-coach sets for its trains. The Metropolitan also had some 4-wheeled stock but the bulk of its trains had 8-wheeled coaches, the four axles being on a rigid wheelbase. Bogie stock did not appear until 1898. However, by this time, a new form of motive power had come to the Underground for in 1890 electric traction was introduced with the opening of the City & South London Railway.

The City & South London Railway was officially opened on 4th November 1890 by the then Prince of Wales, later King Edward VII, between Stockwell and King William Street in the City of London. It was

Right Interior of an 1890 car built for the City & South London service between the City and Clapham. Since the trains ran entirely within tunnels with guards at the ends of each car, announcing the names of stations, it was assumed that passengers would not need to see out. However, in an endeavour to get away from the claustrophobic atmosphere of what passengers had called padded cells, later cars were built with normal depth windows.

the first tube railway in the world and the first underground railway to be operated by electricity. Although it was the pioneer of electric traction in London, the C&SLR almost missed this distinction. When work on the tunnelling of the line was started, it was envisaged that the system of traction would be cable haulage. It was to have been based on the system introduced in San Francisco for the now world-famous cable cars. By the time the C&SLR was opened however, electric traction had been substituted as its traction system, and the company led the way for London's future rapid transit systems. In 1898 the short tube line between Waterloo and the City was opened by the London & South Western Railway and the Metropolitan and District Railways began conversion to electric traction in the early 1900s.

The C&SLR was opened with dc electric locomotives hauling trains consisting of three small carriages. The locomotives were only fourteen feet long. The carriages were specially designed to fit in the 10ft 2in diameter of the original tunnels. They were 27 feet long and weighed only 7 tons. Since they were to run only in tunnels, it was thought that they did not need full-size windows, so only small glazed panels were fitted to the bodysides just below gutter level. There were no other windows. Inside, there were longitudinal benches fitted with buttoned upholstery up to the base of the glazed panels. Entrances for the cars were provided at the ends, where double sliding doors gave access to open platforms. The platforms had gates which were closed between stations and opened by 'gatemen' to allow passengers to board and alight. The lack of proper windows meant that the gatemen had to announce the stations to the passengers and the noise level was such that the names had to be shouted if people were to hear them.

In 1900 the C&SLR opened extensions to Clapham Common in the south and to Moorgate in the north. The Moorgate extension allowed the original terminus at King William Street to be abandoned, being replaced by a station at Bank. A further extension of the line to Angel was opened in 1901 and another to Euston was opened in 1907.

In spite of its primitive technology, the C&SLR, which is now part of the Northern (via Bank) line, was regarded as a success and it encouraged the building of other tube lines. In 1900 the Central London Railway was opened between Shepherd's Bush and Bank, cutting right across the central area within the Circle line and connecting the shopping district of Oxford Street with the financial district in the City. It also provided access to the then fashionable suburb of Shepherd's Bush. Like the C&SLR, this line opened with electric locomotives hauling passenger cars, but the trains were up to seven cars long. However, after only three years of operation the locomotives were

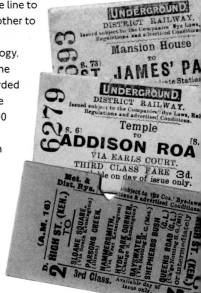

Left Russell Square, Piccadilly line, opened in 1906. The building was designed by Leslie Green, with distinctive terracotta cladding and arched first floor windows, which was standard for stations on tube railways under the financial control of Charles Tyson Yerkes.

replaced because of their excessive vibration. Multiple-unit traction then became the standard system of operation. This provided drivers' cabs at each end of each train and eliminated locomotive changing at termini. With a service frequency of up to 30 trains per hour, the Central London Railway became London's first tube rapid transit railway.

More tube lines appeared following the opening of the Central London. The Bakerloo, Piccadilly and Hampstead lines were all opened during 1906-7. They formed the cores of the much longer lines now seen today. The Bakerloo was the first of the three to open, on 10th March 1906. It was originally known as the Baker Street and Waterloo Railway, although it originally ran from Baker Street to the station now known as Lambeth North and was extended to Elephant & Castle in August 1906. Extensions of the line to the north west were opened in stages over the next ten years, reaching Edgware Road in June 1907, Queen's Park and Willesden Junction in 1915 and Watford in 1917. Between Queen's Park and Watford the Bakerloo trains ran over the new tracks specially constructed by the London & North Western Railway next to its main line for its own suburban electric service. At that time the Bakerloo was the longest of the tube lines and remained so until the opening of the Piccadilly extensions in 1932-33.

The Piccadilly line was opened as the Great Northern, Piccadilly and Brompton Railway in December 1906. It ran between Finsbury Park and Hammersmith and had a small branch from the main route at Holborn to Aldwych opened in November 1907, which remained a minor spur until closure in 1994.

The Hampstead line was the last of the lines to be opened as a result of the tube railway boom of the 1900s.

It opened between Charing Cross and Golders Green (with a branch to Highgate) in 1907 and eventually became part of the Northern line after being combined with the rebuilt C&SLR.

By the time they were opened, the Bakerloo, Piccadilly and Hampstead lines were all owned by the Underground Electric Railways of London Ltd (UERL) which by now had also taken over the District Railway. The three tubes were formed into a common company called the London Electric Railway (LER). The UERL also absorbed the Central London and the C&SLR in 1913.

The three Yerkes tubes began their operations with multiple unit trains. As on the older tubes, the cars had open end entrances with iron lattice or grille gates. The first Metropolitan and District electric stock also had open ends but they quickly introduced enclosed entrances and middle doors to both improve weather protection and speed up station stops. The tube lines began introducing these improvements from 1915 and, from the early 1920s, they introduced air operated sliding doors on all new tube cars.

Both the Central London and the C&SLR had slightly smaller tunnels than the three LER tubes. A start was made towards standardisation during the 1920s when the C&SLR was enlarged to match the LER tunnel size and was extended south to Morden. The improvements to the C&SLR were designed to combine the line with the Hampstead. The two lines were connected at Kennington and Camden Town and the Hampstead line was extended from Golders Green to Edgware.

The Central London Railway was extended from Bank to Liverpool Street in 1912 and to Ealing Broadway in 1920 over a line built in a partnership with the Great Western Railway,

but it had to wait until 1938 for its tunnels to be enlarged to normal tube size. This was done as part of the plans for long eastern and western extensions to Epping, Hainault, Ongar and West Ruislip. The second world war delayed these but they were opened by the end of the 1940s.

The idea of extending the tube lines to create suburbs and thus generate custom had begun in 1907 with the opening of the Hampstead tube to the open countryside at Golders Green. It was thought, rightly, that residential development would occur if good transport were provided. The idea had been imported from the United States with Yerkes and his engineers, who had seen the same phenomenon in New York and Chicago.

The Piccadilly line was perhaps the classic example of the Underground Company's ideal of a tube line extended to serve the new suburbs, thus tapping new demand to fill the under-utilised tunnels through the central area. This line was substantially extended in the early 1930s to the west over two District line branches, whilst breaking new ground to the north with an extension part in tunnel and part on (or above) the surface.

The extension to Oakwood was the last under independent ownership; four months later the modest further extension to Cockfosters was the first to open under the auspices of the new London Passenger Transport Board, on 31st July 1933.

In 1933 the London Passenger Transport Board was appointed by the government to take over the operation of the Underground railways, bus and tram services over a wide area of London's catchment, and the name London Transport appeared for the first time on buses and trains. The LPTB soon hatched the 1935-40 New Works Plan, a programme of works which included a new tube line between Baker Street and Finchley Road to relieve the Metropolitan's worst bottleneck, the extension of the Northern north of Highgate and the Central line extensions already mentioned. Much new rolling stock was acquired, including the 1938 tube stock which was withdrawn from the Underground in 1988 and some of which is still in use on the Isle of Wight.

Following the Second World War a new government embarked on a major nationalisation programme, which in 1948 included virtually all the railways in Britain. London

In the 1920s Tube lines were extended to fill the gaps not served by the main line railways. Stations at first followed traditional architectural practice, as at Hendon Central on the Hampstead tube, seen with a train of Standard stock.

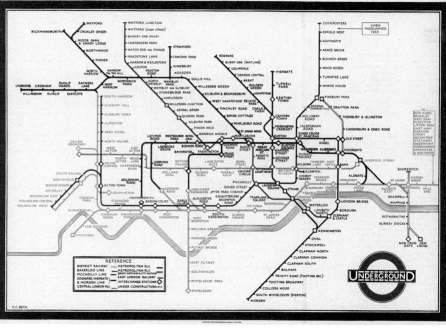

Once built, the Underground needed to constantly remind people of its existence and convenience, especially outside the rush hours when trains were running empty. The Underground's bullseye appeared on book matches as well as the more familiar map, redrawn by Henry Beck in diagrammatic form to make the system easier to understand.

Transport outwardly remained much as before but post war shortages delayed implementation of the New Works Plan, and some key elements, including the extension of the Northern line to Alexandra Palace and Bushey Heath, were abandoned entirely.

The next new venture was the Victoria line, the first Underground line to be fully equipped for automatic train operation. This was opened in stages between 1968 and 1971, after many planning delays and paring station specification to a minimum as a cost-saving exercise, causing passenger congestion in later years.

A further new line, the Jubilee, opened in 1979 when the Stanmore branch of the Bakerloo was joined to a new tube built between Baker Street and Charing Cross. It opened in 1979. After many false starts, work commenced late in 1993 on an important extension to serve London's former Docklands, which was opened in late 1999 in time to serve London's new millennium celebrations at North Greenwich.

In 1977 the Piccadilly line was extended to Heathrow Airport. The building of a new terminal (Terminal 4) later became necessary and it was decided to include a link for the Underground in the form of a single-track loop extension to the Piccadilly line. This opened in 1986. Although a straight section was provided in the loop for a future Terminal 5 station, when this terminal was finally proposed in the 1990s it was at Perry Oaks, on the western side of the airport and remote from the tunnel. Consequently a new branch was constructed, opening on the same day as the terminal itself in March 2008.

The East London line has been an element of the Underground since the mid 19th Century, but in many ways failed to reach its true potential as a link in an orbital railway. Keen to develop orbital traffic and reduce congestion, Transport for London closed the line in December 2007 to equip it as part of the new London Overground network, bringing Underground service standards to surface lines operated, in the main, as part of the national rail network.

Following nationalisation political influence continued to impact the management of the Underground. In 1970 control of the network passed to the Greater London Council, only to revert to the government in 1984 when London Regional Transport was brought into life shortly before the Greater London Council was abolished altogether. London Underground Ltd was formed as a subsidiary of LRT on 1st April 1985. In 2003 London Underground again became part of local government, but this time only as an operator, the stewardship of assets having been passed to the newly-formed Infrastructure Companies, in private ownership. However, only five years later part of the asset renewal and maintenance role reverted to public ownership after the collapse of one of the new companies.

London Underground has also had a distinguished history in the development of its public image and its approach to art. The best known symbol of the

Right Events that could be reached by Underground were advertised within the cars. It was on the design of these small posters that many designers later to be famous cut their teeth.

Below right Good design remains a feature of Underground publicity today.

Underground is the bar and circle. About 1908, the first version of the now familiar symbol, but with a solid red disc, appeared on station platforms as a way of displaying the station name. In 1916, a new corporate typeface was introduced on the Underground, designed by Edward Johnston and used on new signs and publicity. It has remained in use with only minor modification to this day — as clear and crisp as ever — a tribute to the simplicity and clarity of the original design. Johnston also redesigned the bar and disc symbol so that it became the bar and circle device similar to that used today. During the expansion of the system in the 1920s and 1930s it was incorporated into exterior designs and is now universally used to say 'Here is the Underground'. The famous Underground line diagram has also become an internationally acknowledged masterpiece and its principles have been adopted by transport organisations throughout the world. It was originally designed by Harry Beck in 1931 and published two years later.

London Underground became renowned throughout the world as a leader in the use of high quality art in its publicity before World War 1, and this continued throughout the 1920s and 1930s with work by eminent artists Graham Sutherland, E. McKnight Kauffer and many others. The posters became so popular that they have been reproduced for sale to the public, and some have been revived for modern publicity purposes. Today the tradition continues and has been supplemented by programmes displaying a variety of art forms across the system. 'Poems on the Underground', a series of short verses displayed on advertising sites in the trains, have also relieved the monotony of tube travel over many years.

As a shopkeeper will provide an attractive window display to entice customers inside to buy his goods, so the Underground must provide attractive stations to persuade customers to sample its services. The diverse origins of many of the lines forming the Underground have left a legacy of variety in station design in addition to the range of site needs ranging from deep-level tube lines in the centre of the city to stations serving small country towns in the outer suburbs. Since the early years of the twentieth century the street access to every station has been marked by the world-famous Underground logo, a universal sign of the quality to be expected.

The initial station buildings opened with the first underground railway on the north side of the Circle line between Paddington and Farringdon have all been replaced or extensively modified. However, a good impression of what they were like can be seen at Bayswater, where the original building of 1868 is still in use and still in some respects as built, and on the Circle line platforms at Baker Street. All platforms on the sub-surface lines are close

enough to the surface to allow access by stairs.

Many of the Circle stations were built in an open cutting and originally provided with an arched overall roof. One of the best remaining examples can be seen at Paddington, where the platforms have been restored to near their original condition. The air space over stations like this can become a lucrative asset if developed as a property site. Early examples were the flats over Baker Street station known as Chiltern Court, which were completed in 1929, and London Underground's own headquarters at St James's Park which were opened the same year.

When an extra pair of tracks was built in 1866 between King's Cross and Moorgate to cope with main line rail traffic wishing to use the Metropolitan's route, the stations had to be enlarged. Farringdon and Barbican (then Aldersgate) are still much as they were then and Farringdon still sports its magnificent twin overall roof.

As lines were extended into the suburbs and the open air, so stations developed in a similar style to those of other railways. The buildings at Rickmansworth are typical of the 1880s expansion period on the Metropolitan, whilst the later suburban style of the 1920s can be seen at Croxley. The country flavour is much more apparent here, especially when compared with the Portland stone faced frontages of Charles Holden for the tube lines of the era, visible between Clapham South and Morden.

The District also extended into the suburbs, particularly in west London, but few of the original station buildings have survived, most having been rebuilt during the 1930s. One which is still much as originally built is North Ealing (now served by the Piccadilly line), which dates from 1903. Here the original station house incorporated a first floor flat built for the District Inspector. In the 1940s, the Northern and Central lines were extended over former LNER tracks, and many of the original stations, dating from Victorian times, still exist, each branch with its own distinctive architecture.

Left Croxley and Watford were built in this style by the Metropolitan Railway for its new branch line opened in 1925. A similar style was adopted for stations on the Stanmore branch, opened in 1932.

Right Clapham South was the first station to be opened on the City & South London Railway's extension from Clapham Common to Morden in 1926. All were built to the designs of the architect Charles Holden.

Architect Leslie Green has already been mentioned. He was responsible for the deep-red terracotta tiled station frontages for the new lines and extensions between 1906 and the First World War. Excellent examples of these include Mornington Crescent, Russell Square and Gloucester Road. At platform level the station name was incorporated into the decorative tiling, and each station used different patterns and colours of tiling, enabling regular passengers to recognise their stop without the need to read the (then infrequently spaced) names. The bar and disc signs appeared on platforms from about 1908 and in 1937 a frieze was added repeating the station name along the length of the platform.

The expansion of the tube lines in the 1920s and 1930s created a new era for station design in London. Such was the quality of the designs introduced during this period that many of the buildings are now 'listed' and cannot be altered without good cause. The Portland stone buildings of the southern end of the Northern line have already been mentioned, and further examples of Holden's first Underground style are to be seen at Hounslow West and Ealing Common. Another 1920s station entrance style, with elements of the Georgian and Roman, by the

Right The District line terminus at Ealing Broadway features an ornate steel overall roof structure. Recent renovation here has seen restoration of the earliest 'bullseye' variant, with its filled-in circle.

Left North Ealing was built on the District Railway's branch from Ealing Common to South Harrow and opened in 1903. District trains were replaced by those of the Piccadilly line in 1932.

Left The original facade of the Great Northern Piccadilly & Brompton Railway's Gloucester Road station was built to the designs of Leslie Green and opened in 1906. Many of these terracotta facades still survive, including some which are no longer in use as station entrances.

Below Completed in 1928, Burnt Oak was built to the designs of Stanley Heaps.

Right Regarded as one of the finest examples of the architect Charles Holden, Southgate was opened in 1933 The building survives in almost the same state as it was opened, together with the vintage road sign post outside.

Bottom right Charles Holden's Arnos Grove of 1932.

Underground's own architect, Stanley A. Heaps, can be seen north of Golders Green - Brent Cross and Burnt Oak being excellent examples.

The early 1930s produced the fine brickwork surface structures seen along the western and northern ends of the Piccadilly line. Southgate, Arnos Grove, Northfields, Oakwood, Sudbury Hill and Sudbury Town all show the large round or rectangular surface buildings typical of this time.

The Central line extensions mark the next big stage in the architectural development of the Underground. Opened in the 1940s, various modern designs appeared, notably at Hanger Lane, Loughton, Wanstead, Redbridge

and Gants Hill. Unfortunately not all of these new structures stood up well to weathering, and the elegant curved platform canopies which originally adorned the west end of the line were demolished in the early part of this century. Blackhorse Road, the only new surface building on the Victoria line when it opened, offers a fine example of 1960s thinking.

A startlingly refreshing new station was built at Hillingdon in the early 1990s as a result of the A40 road construction which obliterated the site of its predecessor: this was the first to have specific lift provision for the mobility-impaired from the outset.

Stations for the Jubilee line extension through the Docklands area have broken completely new ground for the network. Based on the concepts used for the Hong Kong Mass Transit railway, they are designed to provide space rather than elaborate finishes. Most have two ticket hall areas, and generally are constructed in huge rectangular

Above The rebuilt Rayners Lane station was opened in 1938. The high-ceilinged booking hall is a feature of many of the Piccadilly line suburban stations.

Left The present station at Northfields was opened in 1932 on the Hounslow branch of the District Railway. Piccadilly line trains shared the line from 1933 until 1964 when they took sole possession.

Bottom left The dramatic bus station at the forecourt of Newbury Park station was opened in 1949 when Underground services started running to Hainault.

boxes, rather than being bored through the ground. Combined with the employment of eminent architects, the result has been spectacular, with some daylight visible through to platform level in a few cases.

Over the past two decades, all ticket halls have been modified to provide improved ticketing facilities, and most have had automatic gates fitted. Fire safety precautions have also had an impact on appearances, often to provide detection and alarm systems, and always to remove melamines and other materials having unsatisfactory fire performance. Similarly, the need for security and monitoring equipment has impinged on stations. Given the large number of sites of special architectural importance on the Underground, these programmes have had to be progressed sensitively.

Left The present ticket hall at White City station on the Central line was opened in 1948.

Below Hillingdon received a brand new station in 1993, featuring tubular steel and glass.

Left Stratford station was transformed for the coming of the Jubilee line, the architecture forming a gateway to the tantalising 'Docklands experience' beyond.

Below Not an airport terminal, but the ticket hall at the west end of Canary Wharf. The new stations on this line bear little resemblance to their forebears. They make a bold statement to the prospective customer, yet most have simple and functional finishes. They have dual access for safety and to widen their catchment and, above all, space – space to move, to give flexibility and to allow for the future.

Right The dramatic entrance to Canary Wharf station, opened in September 1999. A bank of escalators leads down to the large ticket hall.

The PPP contracts provide for a comprehensive programme of station refurbishments and modernisation. This work started in 2005, and is providing a high standard of finishes, increased security equipment and much improved passenger information systems. Work takes several months to complete at each location, and of necessity, it will take several years for all stations to benefit.

Over the years many stations have been expanded to cope with vast increases in passenger numbers. One of the biggest schemes took place at King's Cross recently to provide new ticket halls and major improvements to access between the various lines and to street and main line railway facilities. Besides relieving serious congestion within the station, the works enabled the Underground to handle expected new traffic from the Eurostar international services (moved from Waterloo to St Pancras in November 2007), the high speed domestic services operating on the same line from 2009, and from the main line 'Thameslink' enhancements which come in between 2011 and 2015.

Another recent reconstruction has been Wembley Park, opened in 2006 ahead of the opening of the new national football stadium. The work has provided a 70% increase in ticket hall capacity, now capable of handling 37,500 passengers each hour, and new direct links to the stadium approaches.

A further departure from past practice has been the construction of Heathrow Terminal 5 on the Piccadilly line. This station is owned and operated by the airport operator, BAA, and together with the entire extension was funded through a Private Finance Initiative. The platforms are alongside those serving Heathrow express, and together are an integral part of the terminal building itself, providing superb access for airline passengers, staff and visitors.

Above right The station building at Hounslow East was replaced by a bold new ticket hall in 2005.

Right To cope with the demands of new main line services at Kings Cross and St Pancras, reconstruction of the Underground station was initially planned in 1996. In May 2006 the first of two completely new ticket halls opened under the forecourt of St Pancras.

Above The new face of the Underground at Wembley Park – for the first time matchgoers to the new stadium can flow unhindered from the station via an underpass.

Left The original, rather modest, facade of Brixton station has been replaced by this bold statement as part of a project to ease passenger flows.

Trains

London Underground passenger trains have historically been powered by dc electricity at a nominal 630 volts, using an unusual four-rail system (with an insulated negative return rail in the centre of the track), although provision is now being made for an upgrade to 750 volts in some areas. Most fleets have both power and trailer cars, although some have only power cars. There are also works locomotives which can be powered by batteries, and a few using diesel engines.

Trains generally use compressed air for brakes, door operation and other ancillary equipment, while lighting and electrical control circuits operate at various voltages, generated locally on each train. From 2009, all stock will have electrically-operated doors as these provide the ability to control door movement far more precisely, and give greater protection against passengers becoming trapped in closing doors.

The trains' air brakes were originally controlled by a solely pneumatic system, but this was inherently unsuitable for intensive stop-start operations, and from the mid 1930s electric control was used for normal service braking, with pneumatic control retained for the fail-safe emergency brake. The 1973, 'D' and all subsequent stocks have a fail-safe form of electrical control for the air brake, and the pneumatic control, present from the very earliest passenger trains, was omitted for the first time.

Trains built from the mid 1960s onwards use regenerative braking to supplement the air-applied friction brakes, thus reducing the consumption of brake blocks and, importantly, generation of dust. Because of the unrefined nature of the power supply, the current generated by electrical braking had to be wasted as heat by resistors under the train on most stocks, However, from the 1992 stock trains have been capable of feeding the current back into the track, and the Central line was the first to benefit when the line's power feeding arrangements were upgraded in the mid 1990s. This is an important development to reduce energy consumption, and reduce tunnel temperatures in the summer, both of which have become critical issues in the last few years.

The shape and size of the trains is dictated by the size of tunnels and station platform lengths. There are two basic types – subsurface and tube (this latter title is widely used to describe the Underground generally, although strictly it does not apply to all lines). The subsurface trains are similar in size to 'main line' trains in Britain, and are restricted to the lines around the Circle, whose tunnels were constructed by cut and cover methods, housing two tracks. These were generally the first sections to be built: most subsequent lines (from 1890 onwards) were bored through the ground to avoid surface disruption, to a small diameter and accommodating only a single track in each bore. Tube trains are therefore significantly smaller.

Because of tunnel operation, the trains have always used the latest techniques to ensure easy evacuation in emergency and high standards of fire safety. Improvements in fire technology have led to all pre-1990s trains undergoing refurbishment, with new interiors and in some cases new wiring too. The opportunity was also taken to provide better communications and information systems and, in trains with more than a few years' residual life, to provide a new interior layout and radically improved finish. The exteriors were painted in a new livery, obliterating the aluminium which had become weathered and pitted,

and resisting graffiti much more effectively. So successful was this process that the majority of passengers believed refurbished trains to be new, rather than having typically twenty years' service behind them.

One-person operation was introduced with automatic trains on the Victoria line when it opened in 1968, and then spread to most other lines by converting existing trains through the 1980s. On the Central and Northern lines the trains had too little life left to justify the high costs of conversion, and guards remained on these lines until 1995 and 1999 respectively, as new trains were commissioned.

Guards had, on most stocks, operated from the gangway at the leading end of the last car (the gangway being available as a normal doorway for passengers when elsewhere in the formation). Conversion to one person operation involved moving the door, heating and lighting controls to the driving cab, and on tube lines the provision of a radio alarm system to alert the Line Controller to a driver becoming incapacitated. Stations served by one-person trains were also provided with mirrors and closed circuit television to enable the Operator to control the doors safely, but trains built since 1990 have been provided with in-cab television instead.

Tube trains

The 1967 and 1972 stocks

When the Victoria line was opened in 1968, it was equipped from the outset with automatically driven trains, known as 1967 stock. These trains had wrap round windscreens and panoramic side windows for the first time, and thus looked much more modern than anything seen on the Underground before. Technically there were some advances too, but in many respects they represented an evolutionary – rather than revolutionary – step forward from earlier trains. Internally the trains used plastics quite extensively, rather than the varnished wood and painted finishes Londoners were used to, and although the effect was very 'modern' at the time, the unrelieved greys soon became tired and somewhat dated.

By the beginning of the 1970s, it had been decided to extend the Piccadilly line to Heathrow Airport, and it was recognised that trains with more luggage provision would be needed there. The plan was to buy new trains for the Piccadilly and cascade the 1959 stock from there to the Northern. To make up the shortfall of the total Northern line fleet, thirty trains of 1972 stock were produced, representing just under one third of its stock. These looked very much the same as the 1967 stock, but had seven rather than eight cars, and were provided with equipment for

two-person operation. A second batch followed in 1973, comprising 33 trains; these had certain modifications and were designated 1972 MkII. The intention was that the MkII stock would initially enter service on the Northern line, pending the arrival of the 1959 stock from the Piccadilly, and thus allow early withdrawal of the increasingly troublesome 1938 stock then operating the Northern. The MkIIs would then transfer to the recently authorised Fleet line, actually opened as the Jubilee.

In practice, the Jubilee line works ran late, as did the delivery of new trains for the Piccadilly, and the 1972s spent longer on the Northern than intended. They did eventually provide the initial service on the Jubilee when it opened in 1979, but were later displaced to the Bakerloo, where they operate today. The first batch of 1972s (which became known as 1972 MkI) became depleted over the years as some were converted to 1967 specification to increase the Victoria line fleet, and others transferred to the Bakerloo. By 1996 only 20 of the original 30 were left on the Northern, and these were all withdrawn in November 1998 with the advent of new trains there, some being placed in store in case required for further use elsewhere.

In 1989, refurbishment work started on these trains, with grabrails, seating and flooring colour-coded to the line identity. In practice, only three of the Northern line trains were treated, and these were refitted to transfer to the Bakerloo after running on the Northern for a brief period.

Facing page The 1972 stock started life on the Northern line, before progressing to the Jubilee, and now the Bakerloo. The 1967 stock on the Victoria line is of similar design.

Below A refurbished train of 1973 stock, seen at Hounslow East. These were the last Underground trains built with wrapround windscreens.

The 1973 stock

When it was decided to extend the Piccadilly line to Heathrow Airport, it was appreciated that more trains would be needed, and that additional luggage space was required. It was therefore decided to order a fleet of new trains, which received the designation 1973 stock.

These were the first to have all-electric control of the air brakes, and the first to have six long cars in the formation, rather than seven standard length vehicles. This provided a train about 6 metres shorter than those they replaced, at lower cost but with very similar capacity. Disadvantages included the need for a slightly narrower carbody to cope with twisting tunnels, and larger platform gaps at curved platforms. Luggage accommodation was provided by having more 'stand back' space at the doorways. The trains entered service between 1975 and 1978.

In 1990, with refurbishment of the 1967/72 stocks under way, one unit of 1973 stock received a pilot refurbishment, based on the earlier work but representing a considerable further design advance. In particular, car end windows were provided for added passenger security, and the centre bays of each car were provided with luggage racks and a variety of novel seating layouts. Many lessons were learned from this prototype, and the production version adopted all-longitudinal seating, with the desired increased luggage accommodation achieved by further extending the 'standback' areas by the doorways. This provision proved very beneficial in clearing crowds on the line's busy central section, and gave just enough space to accommodate a standard wheelchair. Lighting was arranged in a pair of continuous strips, and the overall appearance 'cleaned up' when compared with earlier refurbishments. The first refurbished train entered service in 1996, with the programme completed in 2000.

Tube trains of the 1990s

By the early 1980s, rolling stock technology was developing on a number of fronts, and this culminated in the purchase of 1986 experimental stock, intended as a test bed for a new generation of trains for the Central line. Three versions of the stock were produced, each comprising two units of two cars, thus producing two six-car trains. All cars were of monocoque construction, rather than the heavy solebar with lightweight superstructure concept used on all previous Underground trains, and for the first time the sliding doors were externally hung rather than opening into pockets within the body structure. Electronic control of the dc traction motors was used, offering lower energy consumption and smoother acceleration than the electro-mechanical control used on all other Underground trains.

The experience gained was used for the specification of the 1992 stock for the Central line, which totalled 85 trains. Because of tight curves on the line, the longer carbodies used for 1973 stock could not be employed, and these trains have eight cars of conventional length. The passenger doors are wider than used previously, and like the refurbished 1973 stock, all seats are longitudinal. During the development of the design, British Rail decided to replace the 1940 vintage cars on the Waterloo & City line, and a further five 4-car trains were ordered for onward delivery to that organisation as its Class 482. The cars were identical to those on the Central apart from the external livery, which was initially to Network SouthEast standard. Ironically, with the privatisation of British Rail the line passed into London Underground ownership in 1994 and has since been operated as part of the Central line. There is no physical connection between the Waterloo & City and any other railway, however, and the trains have not been mixed. The new trains entered service between 1993 and 1995, and introduced one-person operation to the Central line. They are fitted for automatic operation, but because of initial problems with the new signalling system, introduction of the feature was delayed for some years. In the meantime the trains became the first on the Underground to be driven manually with Automatic Train Protection rather than mechanical tripcocks. The trains on the Waterloo & City received an interim refurbishment during the line's closure for signalling works in 2006.

The 1996 stock (Jubilee line) was ordered before the 1995 trains (Northern), and has technologically less advanced equipment.

The design originated in about 1991 for the Jubilee line extension, and it was intended to buy new cars to mix with the then existing 1983 stock to produce hybrid trains. The new cars were to feature the stronger structure and externally hung doors of the 1992 stock, but were of more conventional appearance to match the older cars. This design was retained when it was decided to withdraw the 1983 stock after a short life, and provide a wholly new fleet. Fifty-nine trains of 1996 stock were delivered from 1996 onwards. The first of the new trains entered service in December 1997; within a few months all of the 1983 stock had been displaced. Each car is of similar length to 1973 (and 1983) stock, and trains initially also consisted of six cars. Provision had been made on Jubilee line stations for the later addition of a further car, and the conversion of all trains on the line from six to seven cars was carried out over the Christmas period in 2005. A further four seven-car trains were also delivered at this time to further increase capacity, primarily to cope with the rising demand from employment and housing around Canary Wharf.

For many years plans had been under development for the modernisation of the Northern line, and a number of possible rolling stock designs were submitted by leading design houses. Some novel features were proposed, including full width gangways between cars. All featured smaller wheels than used hitherto, enabling them to fit entirely below floor level and thus allowing doors to be located anywhere along the carbody. Regrettably, falling income from government thwarted the scheme, and no further progress was possible.

In 1994 the Government announced its Private Finance Initiative, paving the way for public sector undertakings to benefit from private investment, and work started on procuring a new fleet of trains for the Northern by this means. In due course a contract was signed with GEC Alsthom (now Alstom) for the supply and day-to-day maintenance of trains on a daily basis, which resulted in the 1995 stock, the first of which entered service in June 1998, providing a great improvement in travelling environment for customers and staff. The trains, which are owned by the suppliers and their financiers, not by the Underground, were developed from the 1996 stock design, but using some new technology. Outwardly the two fleets are almost identical.

Above The design of new rolling stock for the Jubilee line originally envisaged new cars running in mixed formation with refurbished 1983 Stock cars. Although the plan was later abandoned, the 'conventional' external appearance was retained and applied to both 1995 and 1996 stocks, the former being built for the Northern line.

Left For the first time on the Underground space was allocated to wheelchairs on these trains. In this 1996 stock Jubilee line car perch seats are provided in the spaces, whilst on the Northern line trains, tip-up seats are provided for use when the wheelchair space is not needed.

The first of the new trains for the Victoria line
seen on test at the Bombardier factory in Derby.

2009 stock

The first new trains for the Victoria line since its original construction in the 1960s are known as 2009 stock, entering service on the line between 2009 and 2011. The 47 trains are built by Bombardier at Derby and include much technology already proven on successful main line Electrostar.

The trains retain the eight-car formation of the 1967 stock, but there are no middle cabs, reducing complexity, maximising passenger space and optimising door spacing. Spacious door vestibule areas and the provision of space for wheelchairs also support faster alighting and boarding times at stations on this very busy line.

The trains are both longer than those they replace, maximising use of the available platform space, and wider, taking advantage of the size of the line's tunnels (these were bored to a larger diameter than the earlier tube lines). Acceleration and deceleration rates are also superior to earlier designs, but achieved with greater smoothness to avoid discomfort.

The trains also include low-level lighting in the doorways, and advanced information systems to help passengers plan their journeys, and if necessary to avoid troublespots.

Now the oldest trains on the network, the A stock was built between 1960 and 1962 for the Metropolitan line and is being replaced between 2009 and 2011. The destination display indicates the non-stopping of certain stations.

Sub-surface trains

'A' Stock for Amersham

This stock was devised during the late 1950s to replace a variety of slam-door multiple unit and locomotive hauled carriages on the Metropolitan 'main' line between the City, Baker Street and the affluent Buckinghamshire hills, at the time of electrification of the line north of Rickmansworth. Two batches were built and entered service between 1961 and 1963. The first, designated 'A60' was to provide the fleet for the Amersham and Chesham services; the second (A62) to displace some of the trains from the Uxbridge and Watford services to the District line, and enable the withdrawal of some elderly trains there.

The trains are formed into four-car units, and operate as such on the Chesham shuttle service. On the Metropolitan

'main line', though, they now operate as eight-car trains, the practice of uncoupling units for the off-peak service having been abandoned in the 1980s.

In 1994 a process of refurbishing the cars was started. The line suffered more than most with petty vandalism, and the train interiors had become very scruffy indeed. Some debate took place before the work started, as the trains were already relatively old, and had a limited residual lifespan. As they had a low priority for replacement in the short term, it was thus decided to carry out a limited refurbishment, with external painting, new interior finishes and car end windows, but without the major re-equipping of the saloon that tube stocks were enjoying. The programme was completed during 1998.

'C' for the Circle

The wholly urban nature of the Circle and Hammersmith lines, coupled with the relative design freedom available on subsurface stocks, allowed the C stock to be purpose built to clear large numbers of people from busy platforms, and each car has four double doorways. This feature has proved outstandingly successful in carrying large numbers of passengers over the relatively short distances most use these lines for.

Trains were delivered in two batches. The first, C69, arrived in 1970–71 for the Circle and Hammersmith lines. The second (C77) entered service in 1978, enabling the type to be extended to the District line's Edgware Road and Wimbledon service. The two batches are virtually identical. The cars are formed into two-car units, operating in threes to make six-car trains. These are the shortest trains operating through central London, limited by the length of platforms around the west side of the Circle.

These trains became early candidates for refurbishment and this was carried out between 1991 and 1994.

D78 for the District

Pre-war stock displaced from the Circle and associated services had become very troublesome through the 1970s, and it became necessary to consider replacement. The District was also home to the 'R' stock, an eclectic collection of cars from various vintages, but having a fairly homogenous appearance to customers. A few of the cars had pioneered aluminium construction in 1949, and some were built as recently as 1959, but it was decided to clear all the existing trains out, and avoid the problems of small residual fleets of older trains.

The D stock was designed to operate over the whole of the District except the Wimbledon–Edgware Road section for which the cars are too long, and was technically based on the 1973 tube stock, with some lessons learned. The similarity extends to the use of tube-sized wheels for the first time, and the six 'long' car formation. The trains were provided with single-leaf doorways throughout; this reduced costs but restricted door width and causes some problems with loading times.

The District line operates two types of train. The C stock (above) runs on the self-contained service from Edgware Road and Wimbledon, and is an integral part of the fleet operating the Circle and Hammersmith & City lines as well. These trains were refurbished in a programme completed in 1992.

The D stock provides the trunk District service. This was the last stock to retain the unpainted aluminium finish externally, but in 2005 work started on major refurbishment. This programme included the provision of car-end windows, wheelchair spaces, new passenger information systems and bright interior finishes.

The S stock will for the first time provide a single, homogenous stock for all the subsurface lines. Double doors will be provided on all cars to speed boarding and alighting.

S Stock – for all Subsurface lines

The need for improved performance has led to the development of a single train design for the entire subsurface network. From 2009 these trains will be replacing initially the A stock, then the C stock and by the end of 2015 the last of the D stock cars. As with the 2009 stock, the technology is based on Bombardier's 'Electrostar' train. The subsurface network is complex, and combines intensive service frequencies with a plethora of flat junctions: not a recipe for reliable performance. The mix of stocks historically operated causes problems on the many common sections of track as all trains are governed by the slowest, and differing performance causes 'bunching' of trains. The planned increase of frequencies in coming years will make this factor far more critical than in the past.

The 190 new trains replace 179 existing ones, providing a substantial capacity increase. The trains will be of either eight cars (to replace A stock) or seven (those that replace six-car C and D stocks). The increase of capacity around the Circle line will thus be even greater, providing much

needed relief to the congested stations in the central area. To accommodate the longer trains, platforms are being extended at a number of stations on the west side of the Circle and Hammersmith & City lines.

For the first time on the Underground, these trains provide a through walkway from one end to the other – this helps to even out the loading of cars, and improves personal security. The ability of passengers to stand in the gangway areas also provides more space, and the provision of three double doorways on each car, evenly spaced along the train, helps maintain station dwell times.

The interior layout provides a mixture of longitudinal and transverse seating to optimise the balance of seated and standing passengers, given the variety of urban and longer-distance traffic on the lines concerned. Comfort is also improved by the provision of air cooling, not practicable on the tube lines because the narrow tunnels prevent effective dissipation of the heat extracted. As on the new Victoria line trains, a sophisticated information system provides details of local attractions, and keeps passengers informed of anything which might affect the completion of their journey.

The tunnel cleaning train is used in tube tunnels throughout the network to remove dust which, if allowed to accumulate, could form both a fire and a health hazard. The leading car is adapted from 1938 tube stock, once the mainstay of the Bakerloo and Northern lines: beyond is one of two 'vacuum' cars, inhaling and storing the dust dislodged by powerful air jets.

Engineers' trains

Throughout history, a specialist fleet has been operated to provide vital support to maintenance and renewal work. This usually operates only at night, but late homegoers and those around for the first trains have often been fascinated by the sudden appearance of strange yellow locomotives hauling wagons and other vehicles through their stations.

The fleet is now owned and operated by the Infrastructure Companies rather than by London Underground itself. Vehicles are mainly based at Lillie Bridge (near West Brompton), and Ruislip, although other sites are used as well, including some off the network.

So-called battery locomotives form the backbone of motive power. These are capable of operation from either the current rails, used to get to and from the worksite, or from the onboard battery banks, used at the worksite itself when the current is switched off. Some diesel locomotives are also used for surface operation.

A number of flat and hopper wagons are used to transport materials and equipment around the network, and these are supplemented by an increasing number of specialist vehicles to monitor track condition and carry out mechanised maintenance.

To monitor track condition and alignment, the Underground built a track recording train in the late 1980s. The driving motor cars at each end are two of twelve prototype 1960 stock cars built for the Central line; the middle car was converted from 1973 Piccadilly stock.

Above Between 1938 and 1974 many of these battery locomotives were built to a virtually identical design. They can use both mains electricity from the track and battery power, and are invariably used in pairs, marshalled at either end of the works train.

Below Originally purchased for use in the construction of the Jubilee line extension, this train of diesel loco and wagons is now available for general use.

 # Lines

Bakerloo line

Elephant & Castle to Harrow & Wealdstone.

The Bakerloo covers 22.5 kilometres (14 miles) and serves 25 stations.

Since the opening of the first part of the Bakerloo line in 1906, it has expanded, contracted and then expanded again to its present length. From its original northern terminus at Baker Street under the Metropolitan line station, it was extended north to Queen's Park by 1915 and in stages to Watford by 1917. The Watford service used tracks built by the main line railway. In 1939 a new branch was built north of Baker Street which ran directly under the Metropolitan line to Finchley Road, where it rose to the surface and the two lines connected. This allowed Bakerloo trains to take over the Metropolitan's Stanmore service and serve the intermediate stations on the line between Finchley Road and Wembley Park.

Until the opening of the Jubilee line in 1979 the Bakerloo operated both Stanmore and Watford services. However, the building of the new Jubilee tube from Charing Cross to Baker Street and its connection to the Stanmore branch of the Bakerloo line meant that the Bakerloo was confined to its Watford branch. In 1982 the Watford service was withdrawn and Queen's Park became the usual northern terminus once more. However, there were occasional journeys to and from Stonebridge Park to allow access to the new depot there and in 1984 some rush hour trips were extended to Harrow & Wealdstone. The present all-day service to Harrow & Wealdstone began in May 1988, Queen's Park remaining the Sunday terminus until October 1989.

The southern terminus of the Bakerloo is at Elephant & Castle, known to the staff simply as 'The Elephant'. Between the next station, Lambeth North, and Waterloo is a connection to London Road depot. This was once the main depot of the Bakerloo but is now only a minor stabling point.

Originally named Trafalgar Square, the Bakerloo line platforms at the Charing Cross station complex were renovated when the Jubilee line was opened in 1979. The new image marked the end of the subdued finishes of previous decades, and heralded bold new designs which were to be a feature of 1980s station refurbishment schemes.

From Elephant to just south of Queen's Park the line is in tunnel. Among the features of interest along this part of the route are the sharply curved platform at Waterloo and the crossover at Piccadilly Circus. At this station, the two separate station tunnels become one at the northern end of the station where the crossover is located. Trains passing in both directions can be seen from either platform, an unusual sight in a tube station.

At Queen's Park, the line rises to the surface and uses two platforms between the two tracks of the Overground Euston to Watford service. A small depot is provided which is unusual in being divided into two parts. At the south end there is a two-track shed capable of accommodating four trains. At the north end another four-berth shed is provided. This has four tracks, two sidings and two connecting tracks which allow Bakerloo trains access to the tracks to Watford. Bakerloo trains on trips north of Queen's Park have to pass through the shed, a unique experience for passengers on the Underground. At night, one of these tracks is used for stabling a seventh train.

Above The Bakerloo platforms at Piccadilly Circus offer a unique view on the network. The 'back to back' layout is itself unusual, but the single tunnel containing a crossover at the north end of the station allows passengers to see both platforms.

Right The stations between Queen's Park and Harrow & Wealdstone have recently been transferred from Silverlink Trains to London Underground management. A Bakerloo line train is seen at Wembley Central.

Central line

Ealing Broadway or West Ruislip to Hainault or Epping.

It covers 84km (52 miles) and serves 51 stations.

As first built in 1900 the Central line provided a cross-London route along the main east-west axis from the Bank to the western suburb of Shepherd's Bush. It was originally worked with locomotive-hauled trains but became the first line to use multiple-unit traction in 1903. An extension to Ealing was opened in 1920.

The original traction system used a three-rail configuration having a centrally positioned positive current rail, and the tunnels were slightly smaller in diameter than those subsequently adopted for later tube lines. The Central line therefore remained non-standard until its conversion to normal tube dimensions and the four-rail traction system in 1938-40. At the same time the original platforms were lengthened to take eight-car trains. Many of the station tunnels in the central area show evidence of the lengthening work undertaken at that time.

The eastern and western extensions of the line were begun in 1936 but were delayed by the war and not opened until 1946-49. At the eastern end of the line a large loop was formed partly by new tunnel construction and partly by taking over existing railways. Between Newbury Park and Wanstead the tunnels were used during the war to accommodate the manufacture of aircraft parts.

Many of the open-air stations at this end of the Central line were built in the nineteenth century by the Great Eastern Railway. Barkingside still has all its original buildings and contrasts sharply with those built in the 1940s at Wanstead, Loughton and Redbridge. The platforms at Redbridge are the shallowest on the tube lines, less than 8 metres below the road. From 1957 until closure in September 1994 a single-track section of railway between Epping and Ongar was operated by Central line trains.

Below Leyton is one of the stations at the eastern end of the line built by the Great Eastern Railway in Victorian times.

Right and below right Gants Hill was opened in 1948, although the design and much of the construction date from before the war. The long concourse between the platforms, similar to the elaborate stations on the Moscow Metro, gives the station a very spacious feel. A renovation and relighting programme in recent years has considerably enhanced the original appearance.

Ongar remains the start point for measurement of the whole system despite the subsequent closure of this part of the line, distance markers being provided every 200m all over the Underground providing reference points for operators and engineers.

The main line from Epping is joined near Woodford and at Leytonstone by the two connections to the Hainault Loop. South of Leytonstone, Stratford is a major interchange.

At Bank, the next station west from Liverpool Street, interchange is provided with the Northern line, the Waterloo & City line, the Docklands Light Railway and with the District/Circle station at Monument. Bank has some very sharp curves which require quite severe speed reductions.

The straight route of the Central line over the central London section enables the 'hump profile' on which this and other tube lines were built to be seen clearly. Each station is approached on a rising gradient and left on a falling gradient to assist braking and acceleration respectively.

The line rises to the surface at White City. This station was built in 1947 to replace the original station which served the area which was known as Wood Lane. The approach to the open section was via the sharp 'Caxton Curve', named after the street above. It has a radius of 400ft and originally formed part of a loop which allowed trains to leave Shepherd's Bush, rise to the surface station at Wood Lane and then return to Shepherd's Bush. The loop also allowed access to the depot. When the line was extended to Ealing

Above The Central line platforms at Holborn were opened in 1933 to replace British Museum station, and provide interchange with the Piccadilly line for the first time. Today this is one of the system's busiest interchanges. Following a competition held in 1980, artist Allan Drummond was commissioned to design the station's new finishes, representing artefacts in the Museum. The work was completed in 1988.

Right The platforms at Marble Arch were given new finishes in the 1980s. This design, by Annabel Grey, depicts the famous Arch in a variety of different colours and decorative treatments and was completed in 1986. Here, it has been possible to incorporate the platform seats into the design as it progresses along the platforms.

in 1920, the westbound line was on the right hand side of the eastbound because of the configuration of the loop. This situation still exists at White City. Access to the depot is now from the station instead of from the loop. The depot itself was replaced by new subterranean sidings in 2007 to release land for the new White City shopping development. Further west, the lines are crossed on a flyover to return to the standard British left hand running layout. Just west of North Acton station, another flyover provides a

grade separated junction for the divergence of the Ealing Broadway and West Ruislip branches. The branch to West Ruislip runs parallel to a Network Rail line and at Greenford and West Ruislip between Underground trains and those of First Great Western and Chiltern Rail respectively. All the other stations are used by the Central line only. At Greenford, a small bay platform is provided between the Central line platforms to allow interchange between the First Great Western shuttle service to Ealing Broadway and

Above The Central line at Liverpool Street is a typical 1990s modernisation with large areas of white. Closed circuit television cameras are housed in the globe hanging from the ceiling.

Above right The line opened to Bank in 1900, when this was the eastern terminus. To avoid undermining buildings above the platforms were very sharply curved, causing problems of noise and large gaps between the platform and train which persist to this day. When the modernisation of the Central line was first planned in the mid 1980s, consideration was given to realignment, but the high cost ruled this out. The station was renovated over several years, and was not finished until 1998. More recent renovations have mirrored the simplicity of this scheme.

Right The gracefully curved canopy at Perivale station, completed in the late-1940s to the design of its previous owner, the Great Western Railway.

the Underground. A feature unique to the Underground is that an escalator is provided to go up to the trains. It is also the last remaining wooden-tread escalator on the system.

Refurbishment of the station platforms on the West Ruislip branch in recent times has included new canopies and waiting rooms. Between Ruislip Gardens and West Ruislip is a large depot. In accordance with the Underground's policy of always providing two exit tracks to each depot where possible, it has a connection to both stations. A new permanent way depot has been provided adjacent to the main rolling stock depot and there is also a connection to the Metropolitan line at the rear of the depot.

West Ruislip station marks the western limit of the Central line and is the terminus of the Underground's longest possible continuous journey. The route from Epping is nearly 55 km (34.1 miles) long.

Circle line

21 km in length (13 miles) and serving 27 stations, the Circle line connects most of London's main line railway termini.

Almost all of the Circle line service is operated over the Metropolitan, Hammersmith & City and District lines. Only the short sections between High Street Kensington and Gloucester Road and between Aldgate and Minories Junction (east of Tower Hill) are used solely by Circle trains. The line's trains are slotted between services of other lines, making it difficult to timetable and vulnerable to delays by other trains. Its normal service pattern requires seven trains per direction operating at 8 minute intervals on a 52½ minute round trip. At weekends and in the evenings the service widens to five trains per direction operating a 10 minute service on a 50 minute trip.

Facing page top Gloucester Road was opened in 1868, and was briefly the terminus of what is now the Circle line from High Street Kensington, before services were extended eastwards towards Westminster. The space above the station has been developed in recent years, and the opportunity taken to renovate the original Circle and District line platforms with cleaned brickwork and imaginative lighting.

Left The 'C' stock for the Circle line was designed specifically for rapid alighting and boarding, and can clear large numbers of people from busy platforms.

Below Bayswater dates from 1868, and is one of a number of Circle line stations retaining the original overall roof. The ticket hall and platform access stairs were expanded in 1998 to cater for the large numbers of people now using the station, but the short platforms here and at other stations between Paddington and High Street Kensington still restrict the length of trains which can be operated on the line.

District line

Upminster in the east to Ealing, Richmond or Wimbledon with branches serving Edgware Road and Olympia.

The District covers 64 route km (40 miles) and serves 60 stations.

The District line is one of the most complex of all the Underground lines and consequently difficult to operate. Its main section forms the southern part of the Circle line plus a single route eastwards to Barking and Upminster. In the west there is a trio of busy branches to Wimbledon, Richmond and Ealing. In addition, there is a shuttle service to Olympia and a Wimbledon service to Edgware Road. All these services pass through Earl's Court, which has become the hub of the line.

One of the main operating problems at Earl's Court is the passage of the Edgware Road service across the main line from the Wimbledon branch. A flyunder is provided for the westbound Ealing line to pass under the eastbound line from Wimbledon. A flyunder at the east end of the station allows trains from Edgware Road to pass under all the main line tracks.

The Wimbledon branch is served by trains from the main District line as well as those from Edgware Road. The stations between High Street Kensington and Edgware Road have historically been able to accommodate only 6-car trains of C stock, not the longer 6-car D stock trains used on the rest of the District.

At East Putney the District joins the Network Rail branch to Wimbledon. Special arrangements exist on Putney Bridge and between Turnham Green and Gunnersbury to separate the 4-rail LUL and 3-rail Network Rail traction current systems. These automatically ensure a supply to each train as it crosses from one system to the other but without allowing the train to 'bridge' the gap between the two. South West Trains does not run a regular passenger service over the line but uses it for access to the depot at Wimbledon Park. At Wimbledon, Underground trains use their own platforms to the west of those provided for national rail services. East Putney, Southfields and Wimbledon Park stations were owned and operated by British Rail until transferred to the Underground in April 1994 as a consequence of the privatisation of British Rail.

The line to Richmond (once part of the London & South Western Railway's Richmond to Kensington branch) is shared with Overground trains working between Richmond and North Woolwich on the North London line. On its journey from Richmond the line crosses the River Thames at Kew. A similar crossing occurs at Putney Bridge on the Wimbledon branch and the District is the only Underground line to cross the Thames by bridge. At Gunnersbury the Overground service continues towards South Acton while the District route forms an impressive junction with the four-track District and Piccadilly lines at Turnham Green. The line from Gunnersbury to Richmond is owned by Network Rail.

Between Acton Town and Barons Court the Piccadilly line occupies the two centre tracks and the District the two outer tracks. The District stops at all stations while the Piccadilly normally runs non-stop between Hammersmith and Acton Town.

Stamford Brook has an unusual station layout which has four tracks but only three platforms. The two westbound tracks are served from an island platform dating from 1912 which used to be the District station for both directions. Originally, there was no platform for the remaining two tracks, which were once part of a separate spur connecting the Richmond branch with the Hammersmith & City line.

When the Piccadilly line was extended westwards from Hammersmith in 1932 a new platform was provided

The Underground is rightly proud of the rich architectural heritage it owns. Barons Court is an interesting example of an Edwardian station designed in a similar idiom to the many Leslie Green stations on 'tube' lines, but by a different architect – in this case Harry Ford. The 1906 ticket hall was renovated with great care for new ticketing technology in the late 1980s, with many original features retained.

Left Hanging gardens facing the eastbound platform at South Kensington. Commercial development at this station is planned.

Below The Bank-Monument station complex was comprehensively upgraded through the 1990s to incorporate the Docklands Light Railway (accessed direct from both Monument, by way of escalators from the circulating area visible in the photograph, and Bank) and as part of the modernisation of the Central and Northern lines. The high quality finishes used throughout the complex reflect the importance of the location in the City.

at Stamford Brook to serve what is now the eastbound District. The combination of the two platforms provides an interesting contrast in styles which has not been lessened by over 75 years of common ownership.

Near the east end of Ravenscourt Park, the next station towards London, the remains of the viaduct connecting the line to the H&C at Hammersmith can be seen. The District/Piccadilly tracks drop sharply at this point to pass under the centre of Hammersmith. The District/Piccadilly station at Hammersmith was completely rebuilt in the early 1990s as part of a big redevelopment.

Just east of Barons Court, the Piccadilly line enters its tunnel and runs below the District as far as South Kensington. The tunnel entrance is between the eastbound and westbound District tracks. Further east between West Kensington and Earl's Court there are two connections from the District, one to the engineering depot at Lillie Bridge, the other to Olympia just before the underground junction with the Wimbledon branch.

Earl's Court, once described as the 'Crewe' of the Underground, handles five different District line services which split into three branches at the west end of the station and two at the east end. A few minutes' observation

from one of the passenger footbridges over the platforms during the peak period shows just how complex the train service operation can be. The roof dates from 1878, whilst the Earl's Court Road entrance was rebuilt in 1906 in Leslie Green's standard style for the original stations on the Piccadilly, Bakerloo and Hampstead lines.

Once beyond Earl's Court, the line passes through Gloucester Road and South Kensington. Originally the District and Metropolitan each had their own tracks side by side until they were combined at a junction east of South Kensington. At this station there were originally four through platforms and two bays. The southernmost bay has now almost disappeared under the structure housing the Piccadilly line escalators which can be seen from the present westbound platform.

East of South Kensington the line is in shallow twin track tunnel (except for Whitechapel) as far as Bow Road. The gaps in the tunnel roof along this section are a reminder that operation was originally with steam locomotives. Above St James's Park station is the famous address '55 Broadway', headquarters of London Transport throughout its existence, and originally the site of the District Railway head office. Between this station and Victoria is the

Right West Ham station was rebuilt in the 1990s with the coming of the Jubilee line and its connections to Docklands. New platforms were also added to the former London, Tilbury and Southend lines visible to the right, trains stopping there for the first time since the early 1960s.

Below Bow Road lies at the foot of a step gradient as the District line rises to meet the former London, Tilbury and Southend Railway to the east. In 2006 this became the first station to be upgraded by Metronet as part of the PPP requirements.

busiest section of the Underground, carrying over 40,000 passengers eastbound in a typical morning peak period. Between Westminster and Blackfriars, the line was built as part of the construction of the Embankment, and is effectively running along what was once part of the River Thames.

Also of interest is the cross-platform interchange with the Central line at Mile End, the only example of tube and surface interchange at the same level in tunnel.

East of Bow Road the line rises steeply to the surface. This is the steepest gradient used by passenger trains on the Underground, at 3 per cent, although a steeper one exists at the Acton Town end of Ealing Common depot where the exit road is 3.6 per cent.

Beyond this point the line runs parallel with the former London, Tilbury & Southend line from Fenchurch Street. The main line 25kV electric trains run non-stop along this line except for a stop at Barking. District trains stop at all stations to Upminster. All four tracks along this route were originally owned by British Rail but now the District tracks are self-contained and all links with the fast tracks have been removed.

Some remnants of former links can be seen at Plaistow, where a bay platform is used by some District and Hammersmith & City trains. On the north side of the line is a large car dealers' workshop which was the site of the Plaistow engine shed. At East Ham a disused bay can still be seen on the north side of the platform and beyond the station the main line electric trains depot is built on the site of the former Underground depot. A major new interchange has been provided at West Ham to allow passengers access between the District and Jubilee lines, main line services and the DLR Stratford International service, once part of the North London line until closure of this section in 2007.

Two important stations on the eastern part of the District line, both shared with the main line, are at Barking and Upminster. Barking is a major interchange between other rail routes and the Underground. Upminster is the easternmost station on the District and has a large depot beyond it, not visible from the platforms, built in 1958 to replace the old site at East Ham. At the other end of the line the main depot is at Ealing Common, built in 1905 for the electrification of the District Railway and formerly the workshop for the line as well.

Hammersmith & City line

Hammersmith to Barking.

This line serves 28 stations and covers 26.5 km. (16½ miles).

In addition to sharing the Circle line's rolling stock, the Hammersmith & City line shares the route along the north side of the Circle, which is the oldest part of the Underground. The section from Hammersmith to Farringdon was built to accommodate the broad gauge trains operated by the Great Western Railway in the 19th century. This can still be detected today at places along the route which show generous spaces between tracks and in tunnels. West of Westbourne Park the tracks are further apart than needed today and many of the tunnel sections east of Edgware Road are much wider than sections built later.

The main depot for 'C' stock maintenance is at Hammersmith. It was built for the electrification of the line in 1906 and has changed little since, although it will not be required for the maintenance of new trains. It is located outside the station on the east side of the main line.

On the west side of the main line at Hammersmith an office block was built on the site of the former goods yard and, to accommodate additional stabling tracks should they ever be required, the block was constructed on a raised platform with pillars spaced to allow tracks to be laid between them. Further up on the same side there was a connection to the former London & South Western Railway's Kensington and Richmond line, over which the Metropolitan Railway operated services to Richmond via Turnham Green until 1906. This connection was removed in 1916.

At Westbourne Park, the H&C joins the Network Rail Great Western main line route into Paddington. There are no longer any track connections between the two railways but the H&C passes under the main lines and then runs parallel to them between Royal Oak and Paddington. At this point the new Crossrail service will go underground on its journey from Heathrow and Maidenhead towards central and eastern London from about 2017. The H&C platforms at Paddington are structurally part of the Network Rail station and are separate from the Circle line platforms. The H&C and Circle lines join at the junction at Praed Street before entering Edgware Road station. This is a four-platform station where the District line service to Wimbledon terminates. On the south side of the station (which is in

Westbourne Grove, with its fine Victorian station building and attractive red and yellow brickwork visible above the train.

a cutting) is Griffith House, one of a number of offices used by London Underground. The amount of railway property at this point is explained by the former presence of Metropolitan Railway steam locomotive and carriage depots and sidings.

Further along the line beyond King's Cross is a section where two extra tracks, known as the 'City Widened Lines', run parallel with the Underground line as far as Moorgate. These extra tracks were originally built by the Metropolitan Railway to allow local passenger and freight trains to run off the Midland and Great Northern Railways at King's Cross to Moorgate without conflicting with Metropolitan Railway services and to have a cross-London connection via Farringdon to the southern railway companies. Between King's Cross and Farringdon the Widened Lines cross under the H&C and Circle tracks.

In 1982, the Widened Lines were electrified at 25kV and disconnected from the Underground. In May 1988, the connection with the south London routes at Farringdon was reinstated after being disused for many years and dual-voltage electric trains operated by First Capital Connect on the Thameslink route now provide a service between the Bedford line and several destinations south of the Thames with Underground interchanges at Farringdon, Blackfriars, London Bridge and Elephant & Castle.

At Moorgate and Aldgate, facilities for reversing Metropolitan trains are provided in addition to the through tracks. Aldgate is located on the west leg of a triangle of lines connecting the Metropolitan, Circle and District lines.

At Aldgate East an interested observer at the west end of the station can watch the routes being changed for District and Metropolitan trains. Air-operated point machines are standard on the London Underground and these can clearly be heard operating here. The relationship between route setting, signal clearance and train movement is easily visible.

Towards the next station, Whitechapel, is a junction which provided access to the East London line for empty stock trains going to major depots for maintenance purposes. There was originally a station here known as St Mary's, which was closed in 1938. Whitechapel is the terminus for some Hammersmith & City trains.

Below Green Park was once a relatively quiet station served only by the Piccadilly line, but with the advent of first the Victoria and then the Jubilee line, by 1979 it had become a busy interchange. The tiling used on this extension was far more colourful than on the Victoria line, and for the first time was supplied on pre-fabricated panels rather than the tiles being hung on site.

Bottom The first station at Dollis Hill was opened on the already well-established Metropolitan Railway in 1909 to serve new housing. The original structure was replaced by the current one for the opening of the Bakerloo service to Stanmore in 1939, and the whole branch transferred to the new Jubilee line almost forty years later. A Jubilee line train of 1996 tube stock is in the platform: a Metropolitan line train can be seen overtaking.

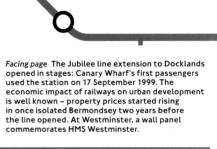

Facing page The Jubilee line extension to Docklands opened in stages: Canary Wharf's first passengers used the station on 17 September 1999. The economic impact of railways on urban development is well known – property prices started rising in once isolated Bermondsey two years before the line opened. At Westminster, a wall panel commemorates HMS Westminster.

Jubilee line

Stanmore to Stratford; serves 27 stations in its 38 km (24 miles). The line runs parallel with the Metropolitan line between Baker Street and Wembley Park.

The Jubilee line was opened to Charing Cross for public use on 1st May 1979. It was made up of two parts: a new tunnel section built between Baker Street and Charing Cross, plus that section of the Bakerloo line between Baker Street and Stanmore which had been worked by Bakerloo trains since 1939. Physical connections for trains as well as simple passenger interchange between the two lines are provided at Baker Street.

The northern end of the line between Stanmore and Wembley Park was opened in 1932 as a branch of the then Metropolitan Railway, most trains just shuttling to & fro and connecting at Wembley with London services. Through services on the Bakerloo started in 1939, when a new tunnel

was opened between Finchley Road and Baker Street.

The section south of Baker Street was opened in 1979 and terminated at Charing Cross, although the tunnels continued most of the way to Aldwych, where interchange with the now-closed Piccadilly line branch was planned by way of the intended alignment to Fleet Street, Fenchurch Street and thence to south east London. When the eastward extension was finally approved in 1993, however, market forces in the blossoming Docklands area drew the alignment across the Thames to serve the south bank with important interchanges at Waterloo and London Bridge (the former serving the classic stockbroker belt of Surrey and beyond), thence to the vibrant new financial centre at Canary Wharf, before swinging northwards to serve West Ham (interchange with District and Main Line services) and Stratford (connections to Essex and East Anglia). This enabled the line to tap in to almost all of the main line rail routes giving access to the City, and feed the new Docklands area.

Diverging immediately south of Green Park, the new alignment has caused the short residual Charing Cross section to be abandoned for passenger services, although it remains available as an emergency 'bolt hole' for empty trains. Further east, another diversion between Canary Wharf and Canning Town has moved the line across the river to the North Greenwich peninsula, adding a further two river crossings to the two that had already been planned. The peninsula was, in the 1990s, mostly derelict, and the intention of the new station was to provide a large car park and bus interchange to serve transport-starved parts of south east London. After construction started the

site was selected for the Millennium Dome, and this added much political pressure to open the extension in time for the celebrations, which it did, with the line opening in stages between May and November 1999.

The new tunnels are to a larger diameter than previous construction, providing space for a side walkway, and have comparatively sophisticated ventilation systems. Returning to the north shore of the Thames for the last time, the line passes through an impressive portal structure, reminiscent of the Thames Barrier, near the mouth of the Lea, to a station at Canning Town. This provided interchange with the then Silverlink North Woolwich service, the Docklands Light Railway and local bus routes. The line then continues

Left The aimed for contrast between stations on the Jubilee line extension is particularly marked on the open air section. West Ham is the only red brick station on this stretch.

alongside the Stratford International branch of the DLR, open in 2010, and passing the new rolling stock depot at Stratford Market just before the terminus.

The architecture of the stations on the extension can be described as spectacular. All have vast tracts of space, and project architect Roland Paoletti has employed world famous architects at the various stations resulting in a statement of importance not seen in the Underground since Charles Holden's designs of the 1930s. Canary Wharf is arguably the largest, although during construction Westminster was the country's deepest and most complex excavation - and with the District & Circle line station suspended perilously at the top and remaining in use throughout! At London Bridge the new ticket hall imaginatively uses the brick arches below the Network Rail station. All of the new below-ground stations have platform edge doors to reduce the impact of draughts.

Stations on the rest of the line have a variety of styles ranging from late-1970s at Baker Street and south to Charing Cross, through late-1930s at Kilburn and Dollis Hill, early 1930s Metropolitan suburban at Kingsbury, Canons Park and Stanmore, to 1920s Metropolitan urban at Willesden Green and 1880 Metropolitan rural at Neasden.

Metropolitan line

Runs from Aldgate to Amersham, with branches to Chesham, Watford and Uxbridge with a total length of 67 km (41½ miles) serving 34 stations.

The Metropolitan line is more suburban in character than the rest of the Underground and it has some semi-fast trains. Only the section south of Finchley Road is in tunnel; the remainder is in the open.

Originally the tunnel section had three stations between Finchley Road and Baker Street but these were closed in 1939-40 when the Bakerloo (now Jubilee) line was opened along the same route but in deep level tube tunnels. The sites of these disused stations can still clearly be seen as the trains make the climb up the gradient from Baker Street.

Baker Street station has seen much rebuilding over the years with the opening of the Jubilee line and the restoration work on Circle line platforms 5 and 6. The whole complex has a combination of 1860s restoration on the Circle, 1930s on the main station, 1970s on the Jubilee line platforms and 1980s on the Bakerloo platforms.

The tunnels between Finchley Road and Baker Street are, for the most part, in single track bores. This is because the first railway along the route was single-track only and doubled later. At Finchley Road the two Metropolitan tracks part to allow the Jubilee line tracks to emerge from the 1939 tube tunnel originally built for the Bakerloo extension from Baker Street. The Jubilee line serves the intermediate stations between Finchley Road and Wembley Park which were operated by the Metropolitan before the 1939

changes. Now the Metropolitan trains normally run non-stop between these two stations. On the west side of the line runs the Chiltern Rail service to Marylebone.

At Neasden, on the east side of the Metropolitan line, is Neasden Depot. This is the main depot for the Metropolitan line and is the largest on the Underground, housing also part of the Jubilee line fleet. It was formerly the site of the Metropolitan Railway works, main depot and power station. After the depot was rebuilt to its present configuration in the late 1930s only a small steam shed was retained. This is still visible at the north end of the yard although the last

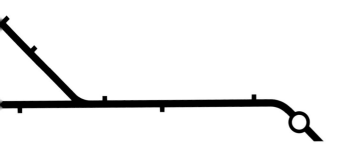

steam locomotives were withdrawn in 1971. There has been much re-equipment of Neasden in recent years, including new automatic train washing machines and a new signalling system using solid state interlocking.

At Wembley Park, north of which the 1932 Metropolitan Railway Stanmore branch diverges, the signal box then installed and equipped with centralised train control still stands at the country end. The control equipment has long since been removed and Jubilee line tube trains now serve the branch, which still shows evidence of its origins. The station itself has experienced successive waves of reconstruction, initially to cope with traffic demands of the Wembley Exhibition of 1924-25, and then with suburban growth and the crowds going to Wembley Stadium. The most recent rebuild was completed in 2006 in preparation for the opening of the new Wembley Stadium. From here as far as Moor Park trains either run fast or stop at all stations,

since four tracks are provided. North of Harrow the fast tracks are shared with Chiltern trains to Aylesbury.

The north western suburbs of London served by the Metropolitan line were largely developed between the wars and owe much to the former Metropolitan Railway's astute combination of 'Metro-land' publicity, its policy of operating a separate land development company and its electrification and improvement of train services in this period. The Uxbridge line, which diverges north of Harrow-on-the-Hill, was built in 1904 and electrified with the main line to Baker Street in 1905. Further electrification from Harrow to Rickmansworth was completed in 1925 and, under the London Transport regime, electric trains reached Amersham and Chesham in 1960.

The Uxbridge branch passes through an area intensively developed with suburban type estates in the 1930s, most of the houses being somewhat cheaper and smaller than

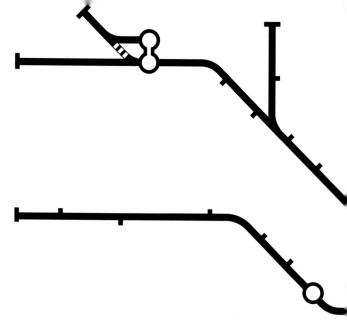

those of the earlier Metro-land developments along the main line. Today only a few fields remain, at the western end, to remind the traveller what the whole area outwards from Willesden looked like before 1920. Most of the stations along this branch of the line follow the style produced for the Underground in the 1930s by Charles Holden, although other architects also had a hand in their detailed design; but Ruislip, which retains much of its 1904 appearance, offers a pleasant contrast.

At Rayners Lane the Metropolitan line is joined by the Piccadilly line branch from Acton Town. Some Piccadilly trains reverse here using a centre siding provided west of the station. This is a typical example of the centre siding used all over the Underground and the observer on the platform can clearly see how it is used and how the signals operate to control it. Few other places offer such opportunities as many of the frequently used examples are in tunnels.

Between Ruislip and Ickenham there is a siding on the south side of the line. This is used both for reversing those Piccadilly line trains which terminate at Ruislip and as a transfer route for stock being moved to the Central line depot at West Ruislip. At Hillingdon, a striking new station was built in the 1990s.

At Uxbridge a set of sidings is provided on the north side of the station, where Metropolitan line trains are stabled overnight. The present station was built in 1938, the original station being now the site of the present sidings. There is a steep gradient into the station and the cutting walls gave considerable problems for a number of years. They had to be specially strengthened in 1954. The station itself is of particular interest. It has a three-track design with the centre track being provided with platforms on both sides. The roof has an interesting clerestory design very similar to that provided at Cockfosters at the other end of the Piccadilly line. There is also a fine stained glass window overlooking the booking hall incorporating the coats of arms of Uxbridge Urban District Council and of Middlesex and Buckinghamshire counties.

The line between Harrow and Moor Park was quadrupled in 1960-61 as part of the modernisation plan for the Metropolitan which included the electrification to Amersham and the introduction of new rolling stock (the A stock) which was to serve for the next fifty years. All the stations as far as Moor Park have platforms serving only the slow lines. Speeds over the fast lines of this section are higher than elsewhere on the Underground, 110km/h being the permitted maximum. The grades are quite steep in some places however and this speed is rarely reached except between Northwood and Harrow.

The picturesque Watford branch – the Metropolitan soars above the Grand Union Canal near Croxley. Proposals exist to replace this section of track with a new link to Watford Junction.

Right Perhaps the epitome of Metroland, the Metropolitan Railway's vision of commuter development, is the village of Chorleywood, where the attraction of direct services to the City had caused a wealthy dormitory area to flourish. By 1990 Chorleywood had the highest number of cars per capita anywhere in Britain. The station opened in 1889.

Bottom Electric trains did not reach Chesham until 1960 – steam being the order of the day from the line's opening in 1889. Seen here is the water tower provided to supply the original locomotives, and the equally disused bay road which once allowed two trains onto the single track branch from Chalfont & Latimer. Most departures from here are now four-car shuttles to connect with the main line at Chalfont; long gone are the ornate compartment carriages and watercress vans.

Just north of Moor Park the short branch to Watford diverges to the right and the tracks are reduced to two from this point. The connections to the Watford branch form a triangle. Trains normally use the southern connection, proceeding from Moor Park to Watford. This branch was built in 1925 at the time of the electrification from Harrow to Rickmansworth. The line was to have reached the main town centre, but the terminus remains about a mile away from the real objective, in a residential estate. The original intentions were thwarted by failure to secure a route across Cassiobury Park. The line, which was expensive to build and produced disappointing traffic results, passes through a spectacular cutting at the approach to Croxley station and then high over a canal just outside Watford.

It was originally intended to run the four tracks of the main line through to Rickmansworth, and traces of the spaces levelled and bridge widths installed can be seen on the northbound or 'down' side of the line. From Rickmansworth, the line climbs steeply through the Chiltern Hills to Amersham, now the most westerly point on the system. The area is quite rural but with scattered areas of development. At Chalfont & Latimer there is a single track branch to Chesham which is normally operated by a single unit of 'A' stock shuttling between the two places. At peak times two through trains operate while the shuttle train is held in the short terminal platform at Chalfont.

The Metropolitan line now terminates at Amersham but a service continues to Aylesbury provided by Chiltern Rail. Amersham station has three platforms, expanded from the simple two-track station of the conventional type originally provided. North of the station a pair of reversing sidings is provided for Metropolitan trains. A little further north still, at Mantles Wood, is the boundary between Underground and Network Rail owned track, interestingly well beyond the point reached by LU trains. The section between Moor Park and Amersham is the only part of the Underground which hosts diesel passenger trains, or any operated by Network Rail franchisees.

Northern line

Morden to Edgware, Mill Hill East or High Barnet via Bank or Charing Cross; serves 51 stations and 58 route km (36 miles).

The Northern line possesses the longest section of continuous tunnel on the system, 27.83km (17 miles 528 yards) between Morden and East Finchley (via Bank). For many years this was the longest railway tunnel in the world.

The line has two main routes across London. Each was originally a separate railway – the City & South London (C&SLR), today's Bank branch, and the Hampstead & Highgate (now the Charing Cross branch). The C&SLR tunnels were built to a small diameter, and these had to be enlarged in the 1920s to match the tunnel diameter of the other tube lines. Some stations show variations in tunnel diameter where platforms were extended to accommodate longer trains.

In some areas traces of the old arrangements still exist. At Clapham North and Clapham Common there is a narrow island platform in a single large station tunnel accommodating both tracks. A similar layout existed at Angel until mid-1992, when a new station opened at a cost of over £70 million. A dramatic traffic increase had rendered the old layout potentially unsafe.

At Euston (southbound City platform) the former C&SLR terminus tunnel originally accommodated two tracks and an island platform. Now it serves only one track and like Angel has a wide platform.

Further south over a section of the line between Bank and Borough the original tunnels were crossed over for ease of construction and led to the station tracks having 'right hand running' instead of the normal left handed arrangement. At London Bridge the southbound track was diverted in 1997 to serve a new platform in a similar manner to the work at Angel. The station had suffered from very congested access arrangements, and the diversion enabled the disused southbound platform to provide a new concourse, with additional routes to the surface and to the Jubilee line.

At each end of the City section there is a junction with the West End branch. At Camden Town the connection is a series of underground tunnels which allow trains to run from either the City or the West End to either of the north London branches of the line.

There is a simpler junction at Kennington. Here a reversing loop (for Charing Cross branch trains) and siding are provided and the line continues south to Morden, the southernmost point on the system.

A variety of services can operate on the Northern line. Trains going north from Morden may run via Bank or Charing Cross to Edgware or to High Barnet or Mill Hill East, a uniquely complex operation for a tube line. At both Camden Town and Kennington there are two platforms for each branch. Cross-platform interchange is provided between City and West End trains at the latter.

The line was extended from the earlier terminus at Clapham Common to Morden in 1926 and the surface buildings along this section are in a standard pattern of Portland stone evolved by Charles Holden, easily adaptable to varying site conformations and designed to show up well when floodlit at night. The whole of this section is in tunnel except for the terminus at Morden. Beyond the station is Morden depot. Although Morden houses many trains overnight, Golders Green is the main maintenance centre. This was also the site of the original terminus of the Charing Cross, Euston and Hampstead Railway when it opened in 1907.

The CC,E&H Railway originally ran from Charing Cross to Golders Green with a branch to Highgate (the present Archway station). It was extended to a terminal loop at Embankment in 1914, which became disused when the line was extended south to Kennington to meet the enlarged City & South London Railway in 1926. The present sharply curved northbound platform at Embankment is located on the former loop. This platform was the origin of the system of automatic warning lights and a recorded 'Mind the gap' message now found at many curved platforms.

Floodgates were provided at Embankment in 1939 where they could be used to close off the under river tunnels should they be breached by bomb damage. Floodgates are also provided at other vulnerable points on deep level and sub-surface lines but few are now needed.

The Northern line has the deepest station below street level on the system. This is Hampstead, which is over 58 metres below the surface. Special high speed lifts are provided here, since it is too deep to provide escalators at a reasonable cost. Just north of the station the Underground system is at its deepest — 67 metres below the surface of Hampstead Heath. Not only does the line have the deepest lifts on the Underground but also the longest escalators. These are at Angel, rebuilt in 1992, and have a vertical rise of 27 metres.

At Golders Green the line reaches the surface and has access to the main depot which lies adjacent to the station. The depot buildings are typical of the 1905-7 style adopted for the original electrification depots and are similar to those at Ealing Common, Lillie Bridge and London Road. Unfortunately, the depot at Golders Green was originally designed for five-car trains: the line now uses longer trains and some tracks in the depot cannot take a full length train, making it difficult to operate. The building boom which took place in the area immediately after the line was opened has effectively precluded any expansion of the site.

Left The Northern line platforms at Tottenham Court Road complement those on the Central (p 40), but with a black frieze to reflect the line colour.

Below left Charing Cross was the last of twelve crosses erected at the resting places of the funeral cortege of Queen Eleanor, wife of King Edward I, en route from Nottinghamshire to Westminster Abbey in 1290. The event is commemorated in the effective black & white mural on the Northern line platforms of that station.

Right Angel station was rebuilt and re-opened in 1992, with a new ticket hall and escalators. The northbound track was diverted to serve this new platform, enabling the original island platform to be converted for southbound use only.

Below The terminus at High Barnet, retaining its country branch look.

Bottom right When the Underground was extended to East Finchley, a new station was built to replace the GNR original. Two island platforms were constructed, the outer tracks serving the line to Camden Town.

North of Golders Green the line is in the open except for a short tunnel at the Burroughs near Hendon. It is interesting to follow the line on foot between Golders Green and Brent Cross stations to examine how in 1923, a victim of its own success, it had to be projected through an area already covered with new houses, some of which had to be demolished. At Brent Cross there were originally passing loops on each side of the station but these have been removed. At Edgware there are stabling sidings next to the terminus and there are still traces of the work done

brick arch viaduct over Dollis Road where the Underground reaches its highest level above ground at 18 metres.

For the extension to Mill Hill East and High Barnet a small depot was built at Highgate including some sidings at the side of Highgate Wood, now also the location of the line's new control room, replacing the 1960s facility at Cobourg Street, Euston.

Mornington Crescent station was closed in mid 1992 to carry out lift replacement and a renovation scheme, but work was suspended by the end of the year through funding difficulties, delaying the reopening until April 1998.

in preparation for an extension to Elstree and Bushey Heath uncompleted at the beginning of the Second World War and abandoned afterwards.

The other branch of the Northern line goes north from Camden Town to Finchley Central, where the line again splits. A single track serves the short branch to Mill Hill East while the main line continues along the very attractive route to High Barnet. The branch to High Barnet was taken over from the main line railway in 1940 and the stations still retain the characteristics of their original owner, the Great Northern Railway. The line to Mill Hill East has a lofty

Right Gillespie Road was the penultimate stop on the original line to Finsbury Park, and the only one to give access to the shallow platforms by means of a ramped subway rather than by lift. The Arsenal football club moved here from Woolwich in 1913, and had gained enough importance for the station to be renamed in 1932 – the only case of a station named after a football club.

Below Once the western terminus of the Piccadilly, Hammersmith station was rebuilt in 1932 when the line was extended further, and again through the mid 1990s as part of a property development. Cross-platform interchange is provided between the Piccadilly and District lines, with lift access to street level and the integral bus station.

Piccadilly line

Cockfosters to Heathrow Airport or Uxbridge. The line covers 72.5 route km (45 miles) and serves 53 stations.

The Great Northern, Piccadilly & Brompton Railway, later known as the Piccadilly line, opened in 1906 between Hammersmith and Finsbury Park. The extensions at each end were largely undertaken during the 1930s. The Piccadilly serves Heathrow Airport using the extensions completed to Heathrow Central (Terminals 1/2/3) in 1977, by a single-track loop to Terminal 4 in 1986, and on a spur from Terminals 1,2,3 to Terminal 5 in 2008. Hounslow West, until

1975 the terminus of the branch, now has its 1920s ticket hall connected to below-ground platforms built fifty years later. Other station buildings of interest on this branch are at Hounslow Central, dating from 1912, and Osterley, Boston Manor and Northfields, all built in the 1930s.

The Piccadilly line from Heathrow passes the line's main rolling stock depot at Northfields and is then provided with four tracks east from there. The eastbound fast track between Northfields and Acton Town is fitted with water

Left Sudbury Town was rebuilt in 1931 as a prototype for the now famous designs on the extended Piccadilly line. It replaced a simple structure built by the District Railway with the line to South Harrow in 1903.

Below The architecture of Barons Court, opened in 1905, is very different to Hammersmith 'next door'. The station had been rebuilt in preparation for the arrival of the Piccadilly line, using the centre tracks, the following year.

At Acton Town, the Uxbridge/Rayners Lane route, combined with the District's Ealing Broadway branch, meets the line from Heathrow. The line to Rayners Lane is in the open throughout, and once ran across the hayfields of Middlesex, but the area was covered by particularly extensive residential and light industrial development in the 1930s.

East of Acton Town, Piccadilly line trains use the two centre fast tracks for the non-stop trip to Hammersmith. Late at night and early in the morning they call additionally at Turnham Green.

The line is in tunnel between Barons Court and Arnos Grove. Of interest along this section is the Leicester Square to Covent Garden portion of the line, which represents

sprays which can be used for braking and adhesion trials for any of the Underground's trains. The branch was once part of the District as far as Hounslow West, and for many years a legacy of compromise height platforms remained to allow a reasonable step between the platform and either type of train. This applies also to the Rayners Lane branch; at Ealing Common and Acton Town the platforms continue to be used by both train types, causing a problem to the provision of wheelchair access.

Right Arnos Grove station, regarded by many as perhaps the classic Holden design, is less well known at platform level. The heavy concrete structures have lasted longer than more recent – and elegant – styles, and little has changed in this view since it was new in 1932. Arnos Grove has three tracks between two island platforms, and is the terminus for some trains.

Below The ticket hall of Northfields is typical of this generation of Piccadilly line stations, offering light and space. Many were originally built with uplighters which were then removed. Several, including Northfields, were replaced in a programme of sensitive renovation work in the late 1990s.

the shortest distance between stations on any line (0.26 km). Between Covent Garden and Holborn the line swings sharply northwards where two separately planned railways became one. At King's Cross there is a single line connection between the eastbound Piccadilly line and the northbound Northern line. Built in 1927, this is the only connection available between the Northern line and the rest of the Underground for stock transfer purposes.

At Finsbury Park there are connections between both tracks of the Piccadilly line and the Victoria line as well as cross-platform interchange. Although the Piccadilly is on 'home ground' in the eastbound direction, the westbound line, with the southbound Victoria line, uses the original terminating platforms of the Northern City line from Moorgate. A centre siding reversing facility is provided at Wood Green, while further north at Arnos Grove station, the first in the open, there is a three-track layout with the centre track having a platform on each side.

Southgate is an unusual station in that it has the only tube tunnel platform on the Underground from which the end of the tube tunnels can be seen. The next station north is Oakwood, which has a connection at its north end to Cockfosters depot. All the Piccadilly stations built for the northward extension of the line from its original terminus at Finsbury Park are built in the late art deco style used by Charles Holden in the 1930s. Many of these designs are now so highly regarded as specimens of the best public architecture of the period that they have become protected structures.

Left Few stations now have the escalator uplighters left, which were almost universally fitted in the 1930s. They have been retained at Southgate, along with the daffodil-shaped concourse uplighters (known to staff as 'the daffs'), partly obscured in this view by more recent signage.

Below The Piccadilly line was extended to Heathrow for Terminals 1, 2 & 3 in 1977. There have since been further extensions to serve Terminal 4 and Terminal 5.

Walthamstow Central to Brixton; serves 16 stations and is 22.5 km (14 miles) in length.

The Victoria line was the first completely new tube line to be built across central London since the tube building boom of 1905-7 and it rapidly became one of the most heavily used lines on the network. It is all in tunnel except for Northumberland Park depot. It was opened from Walthamstow to Highbury & Islington in September 1968, to Warren Street in December that year, to Victoria in March 1969 and to Brixton in July 1971. The line was designed to relieve congestion in the north-east to West End corridor.

From its opening, Automatic Train Operation has been employed on the line, and acceleration, signal checks and station stops are all performed automatically.

The nature of the subsoil south of the Thames makes tunnelling particularly difficult and expensive. The Victoria line extension to Brixton was the first extension of the tube into south London since the Northern line's extension to Morden in the mid-1920s. An important design objective was the avoidance of curves below 20 chains radius, allowing higher speeds than average on the system.

The design of the route also incorporated many cross platform interchanges. Some involved special diversions. At Finsbury Park, the former westbound Piccadilly platform became the northbound Victoria line tunnel and, in the opposite direction, both lines used the former Northern City line platforms where ceilings are higher than usual in a tube station. The Northern City line originally ran between Finsbury Park and Moorgate but was curtailed at Drayton

Below Each of the new Victoria line stations designed in the 1960s had its grey tiled walls relieved by coloured tile panels by different artists – At Stockwell there is a swan design after a local inn of this name.

Park when construction work at Finsbury Park started. In 1975 the line was taken over by British Rail for incorporation into its Great Northern electrification scheme. Cross platform interchange between it and the Victoria line is provided at Highbury & Islington, where reconstruction similar to that at Finsbury Park was undertaken.

South of Highbury the Victoria line tunnels cross to give right-hand running. This allows cross platform interchange at Euston with the City branch of the Northern line. This was another site which involved diversion of existing routes. South of Warren Street the tunnels again cross to regain left hand running.

Cross platform interchange with the Bakerloo is provided at Oxford Circus and with the Northern at Stockwell but at Green Park and Victoria the line is at a different level from that of other lines. Victoria has a pair of reversing sidings beyond the station and at Brixton and Walthamstow two stabling sidings are provided beyond the termini.

A new control centre is provided at Northumberland Park depot, replacing the original facility built at Cobourg Street, Euston, at the time of the line's construction.

Waterloo & City line

Waterloo to Bank, with no intermediate stations. Length 2.5km (1½ miles).

This short railway was London's second tube line, having opened in 1898. It was the brainchild of the London & South Western Railway which by the end of the nineteenth century was already becoming an important commuter route but which, like most of its rivals, was unable to reach the City; then a proportionately more important employment centre than now.

The original wooden-bodied trains survived until 1940 when they were replaced by specially designed tube-sized cars embodying the relatively unrefined technology of the Southern Railway's surface stocks, which had been superseded on the Underground several years earlier. These trains were themselves to survive until 1993, some cars to the end bearing 'Southern Railway' motifs inside, recalling pre-nationalisation days of the early 1940s.

In 1993 the line closed for several weeks for some remaining civil engineering works and resignalling to take place. When it reopened on 19th July 1993, it was equipped with new trains; in effect units of Central line 1992 tube stock added to the Underground order and sold on to Network SouthEast, the only significant difference being in external livery. Further closure took place for nearly six months in 2006 to enable track modifications

and upgraded signalling to be provided. This paved the way for the line to use all five of its trains in peak service, substantially increasing carrying capacity and helping to reduce the traditional long, if patient, queues at Waterloo which characterised morning peak travel on the line for decades. This closure also allowed the trains to undergo an interim refurbishment, during which time they also received standard Underground livery.

The line is wholly in tunnel and physically isolated from all other railways. Until 1990 cars were moved to and from the line by hydraulic lift at Waterloo. This facility had to be removed as part of the preparations for the international platforms for Eurostar services, and the 1940 cars and their replacements had to be lifted by mobile crane.

Uniquely amongst London's tube lines, the Waterloo & City (or 'Drain') remained outside London Transport ownership when LT was formed in 1933. In April 1994 however, with the impending privatisation of British Rail, the line was transferred to London Underground.

Above During temporary closure of the Waterloo & City line in 2006 for upgrading work, platform ramps were provided at all platforms to give level wheelchair access to the second car from the south end.

⊖ Operation

Some of the highest risks of accident arise around the platform-train interface. 1995 and 1996 tube stocks have been fitted with stiff rubber 'buffers' at the carbody ends to reduce the size of the gap – and thus the risk of falling – while earlier trains have been fitted with flexible inter-car barriers to eliminate the gap altogether.

Safety

The operation of railways in Britain is regulated by the government's Health & Safety Executive. This ensures not only that safe practices, materials and equipment are used on the railway itself, but also that working procedures are competently designed and implemented. Staff are properly trained and licensed for the tasks they have to perform while all policy and tactical decisions expressly take into account the impact on safety.

Since the 1980s the Underground has used risk analysis techniques to understand the level of hazards, and to systematically improve safety performance. This approach was helpful in maintaining safety during the major organisational changes in 2003, and all parties have clear accountabilities in the safe delivery of every aspect of operations and maintenance. The effect has been to reduce accidents on an already safe facility still further, and enhance the Underground's position as the safest form of transport in Britain.

Signalling

For much of the Underground's history, trains have been manually driven and signalling has been by means of two-aspect colour lights on lineside signals – green for proceed and red for stop. A repeater is provided where visibility of a signal is restricted – for example on a curve – displaying a yellow aspect to warn of a red signal ahead. On the fast sections of the Metropolitan line, yellow is also used on normal running signals to give the driver longer warning of the need to slow down. Whenever a signal is red, a 'trainstop' located alongside the track is raised, which contacts a lever (connected to a 'tripcock') on any train which attempts to go past, causing an emergency brake application. The layout of the signals is such that any train in this position would be brought to a stand before it collided with a train in the next section.

The signals are operated automatically – a low voltage current is passed through the running rails, which maintains the signal at green. When a train enters the section and short circuits the current, the signal turns red. In areas where the signals need to be controlled manually, including junction areas, this was achieved by levers in a local signal box, or more normally now remotely from a control room. Signals at junction areas are interlocked with each other to prevent conflicting moves being cleared, and with points so that they are proved to be fully set and locked in the desired position before the signal can be cleared.

Route setting has been increasingly automated, so that a move once requiring the operation of several levers became achievable by, perhaps, the pushing of a single button or without manual intervention at all. Originally 'programme machines' were developed for this role in the 1950s. These were mechanical devices using a wide plastic roll containing timetable data in the form of punched holes. The idea was novel at the time, but although many remain in use, their operation is too inflexible for the high intensity and quality of service demanded now. In the early 1970s, a successful trial was conducted at Rickmansworth signal box to use a

Left The need for tight operational control and passenger security has led to the provision of sophisticated control rooms at stations, giving a comprehensive view of all areas, and status indications of the various items of equipment.

computer for the control of the Watford area, leading to a major installation in 1982 at the north end of the Piccadilly line. Although that installation was not without problems, lessons were learned, and all subsequent installations followed the same principles.

The safety interlocking has always remained at local level, originally by retaining the mechanical locking bars used in signal cabins from the very earliest days of the railways, but since the mid-1980s through a fail-safe form of computer-proving, known as 'solid state interlocking'.

Through the tripcock, the basic system outlined above provides a crude form of train protection, but once a train has passed the green signal it is free to continue at any speed. Greater safety is provided by newer automatic train protection systems (ATP) which require a constant 'proceed' signal or the train will stop. Importantly, speed can also be governed, reducing the risk of derailment through overspeeding, and enabling the impact of speed restrictions to be minimised through the certainty that speed will be strictly governed to the desired level.

In addition to the automatic protection of trains, systems can do the work of the driver, and provide acceleration, braking and door opening (or enabling). Like the driver, these systems are always subject to the overriding control of the ATP safety system. The Underground led the world is this field, tests starting on a section of the District line as far back as the early 1960s before full scale trials on the Hainault – Woodford section of the Central Line, and implementation from the first day of the Victoria line in 1968.

A refined version of the Westinghouse system used on the Victoria line was implemented on the Central line, initially with the provision of ATP governing manual driving in 1998, and from 2001 with full ATO.

To upgrade the lines in its portfolio, Metronet selected a Westinghouse 'Distance to go' train control system for the Victoria and Subsurface lines to replace the existing equipment between 2010 and 2015. This represents a further development of the earlier designs used on the Underground and elsewhere, providing the degree of control needed for very intensive operations.

Tube Lines opted for Alcatel's transmission-based control system on the Jubilee, Northern and Piccadilly lines, with installation programmed for completion in 2009, 2011 and 2014 respectively. This system no longer relies on track circuits to detect the presence of trains, but depends on the train providing constant location and status updates, and enables trains to operate more closely together at optimum speeds, but without prejudicing safe separation. The differing basis of the new systems dictates the development of specific engineering solutions where the Subsurface lines meet the Jubilee and, particularly, Piccadilly lines.

Manual operation will be progressively superseded across the network as lines are upgraded, and by 2020 it is likely that all trains will be automatically controlled.

Communications

From its earliest days, the Underground had telephones, but it was not until the 1980s that radio systems were used widely, and for the first time controllers could contact train operators, and communicate while the train was moving.

Communications technology has continued to advance rapidly, and to exploit this a PFI contract was awarded in 1999 to supply and maintain a comprehensive new communications network. The provision is partially funded

The opening of the Jubilee line extension almost doubled the Underground's stock of escalators. Canary Wharf alone has twenty.

through the sale of transmission capacity on the network to third parties, exploiting the routeways offered around London by tube tunnels.

Branded 'Connect', the new system allows virtually any voice or data transmission to take place between all sites, be they fixed or moving. This gives mobile staff additional security and also permits depots and control centres to receive real-time information about any defects on trains in service.

As well as operational communication, customers can now be provided with far better information about services, both while on the network, and elsewhere through internet and the other media.

The 'Airwave' radio systems used by the emergency services are also being linked to Connect, so that all emergency personnel can use their own systems below ground.

Lifts and escalators

The means of getting to and from the platforms are as important as the trains themselves. The earliest stations, in shallow tunnels, used only stairs, but the advent of tube construction in 1890 necessitated some mechanical assistance, and lifts were provided – initially hydraulically powered, but soon mechanical winding was used instead.

The problem with lifts is that they can take only a limited load, and then only in discrete batches. Even while the tubes were still much quieter than now, this began

to cause problems, and in 1911 the first escalator was installed at Earl's Court. By the 1920s the machine had developed into its current form, with a straight step off at the landings rather than one requiring a sideways step at the end. Over the next few years escalators spread widely across the network, often involving considerable station reconstruction. Lifts were retained at a number of stations, however, the deepest being at Hampstead (55 metres).

Although escalators are good at carrying large numbers of people, they are unsuitable for those who have mobility difficulties, or who have luggage, children and so on. Enlightened attitudes towards universal access – and the recognition that a very large potential market was being disadvantaged – led a trend back to providing lifts, but to supplement rather than replace escalators. In 2004 an undertaking was given that by 2010, 25% of all stations would provide step-free access to the platforms, with many further stations being added in the following years.

Track

The Underground had normally used 95lb/yard bullhead rail, but this offers little inherent stiffness and in the interests of good maintenance and smooth running, heavier flat bottomed rail is now progressively being laid. Work on the long programme of completely replacing the track, and its bed, is slowly progressing, but because of disruption (a weekend shutdown is usually necessary to replace a section of track) and cost, this has to be spread over

The 'Prestige' PFI project provided for the installation of ticket gates at almost all remaining stations in 1999–2000. The new gates have much narrower stanchions than the earlier ones, and can be used in restricted spaces.

many years. The work includes the replacement of the old limestone ballast with granite – more expensive, but far longer lasting. Often, track renewal has to be preceded by the stabilisation of earthworks and reconstruction of drains, so even on a short section the work may have to be spread over a year or so to allow new formations to stabilise. Routine track and lineside maintenance has to be carried out in the few hours when trains are not running – often less than four hours' work is possible once the site has been reached. Much of this work is locally based, but materials and heavy machinery are stored at depots at Ruislip, and Lillie Bridge, and at some off-network locations.

Power

Energy is supplied through the third and fourth rails at a nominal 630 volts dc, the insulated return originally designed to avoid electrolytic corrosion. This leaves a legacy of cluttered track – difficult for staff and customers, should detrainment be necessary, and expensive to maintain. Although the cost of radical change cannot be justified, provision is being made for the future uplift to 750v dc on certain lines to improve compatibility with Network Rail on shared sections, and to reduce wastage through transmission losses.

When Britain's power industry was nationalised in 1948 the Underground was deliberately excluded to ensure security of supply. Most of the energy came from the company's own plants at Greenwich (a former London County Council tram power station), Lots Road (Chelsea) and Neasden. The latter was closed in the early 1960s, and bulk power obtained locally from the National Grid, but the other plants were upgraded, Lots Road was converted to use either natural gas or oil and provided the base supply while oil-fired Greenwich was added for peak and emergency loads. The remaining infrastructure gradually became less dependable, and in August 1998 a PFI deal for the supply and distribution of high tension electricity was implemented with a consortium which included Seeboard, successor to the nationalised local Electricity Board for south east England, and now part of French-owned EDF Energy. Lots Road was decommissioned in 2002, and virtually all energy sourced from the National Grid. Major investment in the distribution network will ensure adequate energy for new trains and the enhanced services programmed for the coming years.

Ticketing

The bulk of travel on the Underground is now purchased using Oyster cards, which are embedded with computer chips. Tickets can be programmed for a range of uses including staff passes, and enable passengers to pre-purchase travel even if they use the service only infrequently. The tickets can be 'topped up' remotely by a variety of automated methods, and there is no longer any need for passengers to queue at ticket offices. Oyster cards can be used on all Transport for London services, and increasingly on main line rail services into London.

There is much flexibility in setting fares: the use of Oyster cards enables great savings to be made over cash fares, while off-peak and other incentives can also be offered. Magnetically-encoded tickets have been retained for non-Oyster users, although these now represent only a minority of journeys.

In 2007 a deal was implemented with Barclays Bank, providing a new credit card with Oyster technology and allowing also low-value purchases at shops, reducing further the need for cash based transactions.

 # Future

Helped by London's expanding population, buoyant economy and improving quality of its own service, the Underground has experienced growth in demand for a number of years. This trend is forecast to continue until at least 2020.

As consumers we are also more demanding than our predecessors: although we care more for our environment and we try to look after the less able members of society better than before, we are also fondly attached to our cars, and intolerant of crowding, unpredictable journey times and unpleasant surroundings.

Through the PPP solution and public funding a massive programme of investment is under way to address the expectations of London as a whole, and to replace equipment which is worn out and inadequate for today's needs.

Upgrading the train service

The intention is to improve real and perceived journey times by sustainably increasing speeds and capacity. The Infrastructure Companies have to meet specific performance improvements by target dates, and although they have a free hand in how this performance uplift is achieved, there is no realistic alternative to the complete renewal of most train service related assets. The separately supplied Connect communications system enables the much improved real-time service information available from new control packages to be supplied to customers wherever they are, both before and during their journey, through the use of new media technology.

The Central and Waterloo & City lines already have relatively new signalling & control systems and trains, and few improvements are still required on these lines. The

Facing page The construction of new ticket halls, escalators and passageways at Victoria also provides for new street access from Bressenden Place to the north, which has seen major office and shopping development in recent years.

Left The new trains for the subsurface lines break new ground by having wide gangways between cars. The seating layout has been designed to address the needs of long-distance passengers, and of intensive operation in central areas.

Jubilee and Northern lines equally have modern trains, but these lines are receiving new signalling and control systems, commissioned in 2009 and 2011 respectively, to maximise performance and fully exploit the capability of the trains themselves. New control rooms, with a totally revised layout, will be provided at Neasden and Highgate respectively, the latter in a new building designed to fit well with the local environment and with ecological demands.

The Victoria line still had its original 1960s assets in full use forty years after opening, by which time almost everything needed replacing. New trains and signalling have already been described, and a new control room dedicated to the line is located at Northumberland Park depot

Arguably the greatest change is taking place on the

Subsurface lines – the Metropolitan, District, Circle and Hammersmith & City, which need to be considered together as a single railway network. The homogenous fleet of new trains described earlier will bring greater capacity and service reliability, but will also require physical changes. The greater length of the trains renders most of the in-town sidings unusable, so additional berthing is being provided elsewhere on the lines in addition to that needed to cater solely for the increased fleet. Similarly, at the western side of the Circle and Hammersmith & City lines, platforms are being extended to support the additional car on each train. This is relatively simple at some of the suburban locations, but at those in cuttings and tunnel areas, major construction is needed.

An extensive publicity campaign is designed to inform customers and to win hearts and minds – the benefit of the upgrade investment in future years will be enormous, but building work inevitably causes short-term disruption.

The increased service frequencies required for the upgrade also put pressure on terminal facilities. This will be acute at Barking, where a revised platform layout could benefit interchanging passengers, but construction costs may dictate operational improvements instead. At Rayners Lane, the combined effect of increases on both Metropolitan and Piccadilly lines renders the current layout particularly inadequate, and for which a number of alternative schemes were being studied in advance of work starting on the Piccadilly line upgrade.

A fully integrated control facility is being provided for the subsurface lines, bringing the minute-by-minute management of this complex network into one place for the first time in history.

Improved services are due to be delivered on the Piccadilly by spring 2014. This requires the new signalling and control system outlined above, which will be managed from a new control room similar to those provided for the Jubilee and Northern lines. New trains will be delivered as a key part of the package.

Work is not due to start on upgrading Bakerloo line assets until around 2015, by which time considerable experience will have been gained in implementing new and more intensive services. By the time this line is complete, train service capacity around the network should be 25% greater than at the time of PPP implementation in 2003.

Extending the system

Almost all capacity change on the Underground will be achieved on the existing network. The only extension currently under development is a joint venture between TfL and Hertfordshire County Council to extend the Metropolitan line from its present terminus to Watford Junction, using the alignment of the former main line branch to Croxley Green. Although the lines are physically close on the map, they are separated in elevation in a complex area which includes the Grand Union Canal – costs of establishing the link are therefore high. New stations are planned at Ascot Road and Watford West, with improvements made to the existing stations at Watford High Street and Watford Junction. The new link would make access to the centre of Watford much easier from the west, and reduce road congestion.

The Underground has a significant interest in Crossrail, for which new tunnels will be built across central London so that main line trains can operate from Maidenhead and Heathrow Airport in the west, to Shenfield and Abbey Wood in the east. The enormously buoyant Canary Wharf area in Docklands will also be served; indications are that the DLR and Jubilee services will be struggling to meet demand by the time the new line is due to open in 2017. The line will be served by trains of up to 12 cars, and will require massive new stations on the tunnel section at Paddington, Bond Street, Tottenham Court Road, Farringdon/Barbican, Moorgate/Liverpool Street, Whitechapel and on the Isle of Dogs, near Canary Wharf. The Underground is expected to participate in the operation of the central area stations, but will not be responsible for the train service.

Stations

Over the next few years virtually all Underground stations will benefit from refurbishment, new information and control systems, and improved security measures to keep crime to low levels and support the international drive against terrorism. Step free access between street and platform level will be provided at ever more stations, normally using lifts, and as new trains are delivered the floor height and platform edges will be matched to ensure wheelchair access.

At some locations however this will not be enough. Rising demand and the pressure of new train services needs to be met by radically improved capacity at several stations. Costs for this are very high – usually new access subways, escalator and lift shafts and ticket halls are all required, necessitating property acquisition and demolition as well as deep-level tunnelling.

Victoria Underground station currently handles 80 million passengers a year (more than the whole of

A substantial enlargement of Tottenham Court Road station to cater for passenger growth will also cater for the Crossrail scheme. Two new entrances will be built in front of Centre Point to access an enlarged ticket hall.

Heathrow Airport), and this is due to rise to 100 million by 2016. Even now, the station makes a lasting impression on anybody trying to enter it in the morning peak - the chances are that a wait of several minutes outside the station is followed by a few more before getting through the ticket gates and onto the escalators. To obviate this, the existing Victoria line ticket hall will be enlarged, with a completely new facility added to the north of the site, tapping into the heavily developed area north of Victoria Street, which currently has no direct access to the station. Nine new escalators will be provided, with new subways and new lifts to provide step-free access to all levels.

Similarly dramatic improvements are in hand for Tottenham Court Road, in advance of the vast enlargement required for Crossrail services in 2017. The first phase is planned to provide an enlarged ticket hall with new street entrances, additional escalators and five new lifts to give step-free access.

Camden Town is another location notorious for congestion, especially at weekends when the local markets are thronging with visitors, causing the station to be operated in 'exit only' mode at busy times. A comprehensive scheme had been developed by 2004, but the proposed surface buildings failed to secure planning permission, causing the whole scheme to founder, and adding many years and much cost to the redevelopment. Revised plans will emerge in due course, but for the moment this remains one of the most unsatisfactory and congested locations on the system.

Live information

The combined effect of new trains, new control systems, re-equipped stations and the Connect communications system is beginning to enable a revolution in access to real-time and advance information. Live service information for all TfL services is already accessible by mobile phone and internet, as well as through radio and television. As the upgrade work progresses, passengers travelling through the network will also have access to personal assistance where needed, and be informed of any service problems in good time for decisions about the rest of their journey. Apart from saving time and frustration locally on the Underground, this recognises door-to-door needs of the traveller and supports integration of all travel modes in London.

Cooling the experience

Climate change, more passengers, higher levels of service consuming more energy and the diminished ability of once-cool tunnels to absorb heat have all combined to make summer on the tube an unpleasantly hot and humid experience. Train-borne air conditioning is virtually impossible in deep level tube tunnels because of space constraints and inability to disperse the heat generated, and in any case adds to energy consumption, and so is not an ecologically sound or sustainable solution.

A problem is that the new services themselves cause more heat – to deliver the improvements needed the trains are heavier than their predecessors, accelerate more rapidly and there are more of them. Similarly, new escalators and lifts all add to the energy requirement, and energy consumed ends up as heat one way or another. Improved train braking and better power distribution help to limit the increase, but still leave a net worsening of the problem.

To combat this, experiments are under way to reduce the temperature in stations and tunnels by sustainable methods without resorting to energy-hungry air conditioning. Early results are encouraging, but cannot necessarily be applied to all locations, and much still has to be done.

Chronologies

Present station names have been used in the list. Lines are shown in the order of opening.

Metropolitan and Hammersmith & City lines (including north half of Circle line)

1863 Opened on 10 January as the Metropolitan Railway from Farringdon to Paddington

1864 Extension to Hammersmith with branch from Latimer Road to Kensington (Olympia)

1865 Extension from Farringdon to Moorgate

1868 Branch opened from Baker Street to Swiss Cottage

1868 Part of Circle line opened from Edgware Road to South Kensington

1875 Extension from Moorgate to Liverpool Street

1876 Extension from Liverpool Street to Aldgate

1877 Service opened between Goldhawk Road and Richmond, over District Railway route between Ravenscourt Park and Richmond

1879 Extension from Swiss Cottage to Willesden Green

1880 Extension from Willesden Green to Harrow-on-the-Hill

1882 Extension from Aldgate to Tower Hill

1884 Branch opened from Aldgate East to East London Railway

1885 Extension from Harrow-on-the-Hill to Pinner

1887 Extension from Pinner to Rickmansworth

1889 Extension from Rickmansworth to Chalfont & Latimer and Chesham

1892 Extension from Chalfont & Latimer to Aylesbury

1894 Extension from Aylesbury to Verney Junction

1899 Branch to Brill taken over

1904 Branch opened from Harrow-on-the-Hill to Uxbridge

1906 Services from Goldhawk Road to Richmond withdrawn

1906 Through services to East London Railway withdrawn

1908 Extension from Aldgate East to Whitechapel

1913 Through services to East London Railway re-introduced

1925 Branch opened from Moor Park and Rickmansworth to Watford

1932 Branch opened from Wembley Park to Stanmore

1935 Closure of Brill Branch

1936 All services north of Aylesbury withdrawn (limited service re-introduced between Aylesbury and Quainton Road from 1943 to 1948)

1936 Extension from Whitechapel to Barking

1939 Through services to East London line withdrawn

1939 Transfer of Stanmore branch to the Bakerloo line

1940 Closure of branch from Latimer Road to Olympia

1961 Withdrawn between Amersham and Aylesbury upon electrification of the line between Rickmansworth and Amersham

District line (including south half of Circle line)

1868 Opened on 24 December as the Metropolitan District Railway between South Kensington and Westminster

1869 Branch opened from Gloucester Road to West Brompton

1870 Extension from Westminster to Blackfriars

1871 Extension from Blackfriars to Mansion House

1871 Branch opened from High Street Kensington to Earl's Court

1874 Extension from Earl's Court to Hammersmith

1877 Extension from Hammersmith to Richmond, over London & South Western Railway route between Ravenscourt Park and Richmond

1879 Branch opened from Turnham Green to Ealing Broadway

1880 Extension from West Brompton to Putney Bridge

1883 Branch opened from Acton Town to Hounslow Town

1883 Extension from Ealing Broadway to Windsor over Great Western Railway route

1884 Re-routed from west of Osterley to a new terminus at Hounslow West

1884 Extension from Mansion House to Whitechapel and East London Railway; completion of the Inner Circle (Circle line)

1885 Service between Ealing Broadway and Windsor withdrawn
1889 Extension from Putney Bridge to Wimbledon over London & South Western Railway route
1902 Extension from Whitechapel to Upminster (over London, Tilbury & Southend Railway route from Bromley-by-Bow to Upminster)
1903 Branch opened from Ealing Common to South Harrow
1905 Branch opened from Acton Town to South Acton
1905 Through services on East London Railway withdrawn
1910 Extension from South Harrow to Uxbridge
1910 Some journeys extended to Southend-on-Sea and, shortly after, to Shoeburyness, over London, Tilbury & Southend Railway route
1933 Services on Uxbridge branch withdrawn (taken over by Piccadilly line)
1939 Journeys to Southend and Shoeburyness withdrawn
1946 Services introduced between High Street Kensington and Olympia
1959 Closure of South Acton branch
1964 Service withdrawn between Acton Town and Hounslow West (covered by Piccadilly line, with which the section had been shared).

Northern line

1890 City & South London Railway opened on 18 December between Stockwell and King William Street
1900 Extension north to Moorgate with new station at Bank and south from Stockwell to Clapham Common
1901 Extension from Moorgate to Angel
1907 Charing Cross, Euston & Hampstead Railway opened between Charing Cross and Golders Green with branch from Camden Town to Archway
1907 City & South London Railway extended from Angel to Euston
1914 Extension from Charing Cross to Embankment
1923 Extension from Golders Green to Hendon Central
1924 Extension from Hendon Central to Edgware and from Euston to Camden Town
1926 Extension from Clapham Common to Morden and from Embankment to Kennington
1939 Extension from Archway to East Finchley
1940 Extension from East Finchley to High Barnet over LNER route
1941 Branch opened to Mill Hill East over LNER route

Waterloo & City line

1898 Opened on 8 August as the Waterloo & City Railway between Waterloo and Bank
1994 Ownership transferred to London Underground

Central line

1900 Opened on 30 July as the Central London Railway between Shepherd's Bush and Bank
1908 Extension from Shepherd's Bush to Wood Lane
1912 Extension from Bank to Liverpool Street
1920 Extension from Wood Lane to Ealing Broadway over Great Western Railway route
1946 Extension from Liverpool Street to Stratford
1947 Extension from Stratford to Newbury Park and Woodford, partly over Great Eastern Railway routes
1947 Branch opened from North Acton to Greenford over Great Western Railway route
1948 Extension from Greenford to West Ruislip over Great Western Railway route
1948 Extension from Newbury Park to Hainault and from Woodford to Hainault and Loughton over Great Eastern Railway routes
1949 Extension from Loughton to Epping over Great Eastern Railway routes
1957 Shuttle service between Epping and Ongar taken over from BR upon electrification
1994 Closure of Epping-Ongar line

Bakerloo line

1906 Opened on 10 March as the Baker Street & Waterloo Railway between Baker Street and Lambeth North; extended to Elephant & Castle on 5 August

1907 Extension from Baker Street to Edgware Road

1913 Extension from Edgware Road to Paddington

1915 Extension from Paddington to Willesden Junction, over London & North Western Railway route between Queen's Park and Willesden Junction

1917 Extension from Willesden Junction to Watford Junction over LNWR route

1939 Branch opened from Baker Street to Stanmore, over Metropolitan line route between Finchley Road and Stanmore

1979 Baker Street to Stanmore branch transferred to Jubilee line

1982 Closure of section between Stonebridge Park and Watford Junction

1984 Service restored between Stonebridge Park and Harrow & Wealdstone

Piccadilly line

1906 Great Northern, Piccadilly & Brompton Railway opened on 15 December between Hammersmith and Finsbury Park

1907 Branch opened from Holborn to Aldwych

1932 Extension from Hammersmith to South Harrow over District Railway route

1932 Extension from Finsbury Park to Arnos Grove

1933 Extension from Acton Town to Hounslow West over District Railway route

1933 Extension from South Harrow to Uxbridge over District Railway route

1933 Extension from Arnos Grove to Cockfosters

1975 Extension from Hounslow West to Hatton Cross

1977 Extension from Hatton Cross to Heathrow (Terminals 1, 2, 3)

1986 Single track loop extension at Heathrow to serve Terminal 4

1994 Closure of the Aldwych Branch

2008 Extension from Heathrow (Terminals 1, 2, 3) to Terminal 5

Victoria line

1968 Opened on 1 September between Walthamstow Central and Highbury & Islington; extended to Warren Street on 1 December

1969 Extension from Warren Street to Victoria

1971 Extension from Victoria to Brixton

Jubilee line

1979 Opened on 1 May between Charing Cross and Stanmore, over Bakerloo line route between Baker Street and Stanmore

1999 Extension opened in stages from Green Park to Stratford; closure of Charing Cross to Jubilee line services